WHISPERI[]

O[]

THE ANGLESEY CATAMANUS INSCRIPTION
STRIPT BARE

A DETECTIVE STORY

by

CHARLES THOMAS

Oxbow Books

Published by
Oxbow Books, Park End Place, Oxford OX1 1HN

ISBN 1 84217 085 6

A CIP record of this book is available from the British Library

This book is available direct from
Oxbow Books, Park End Place, Oxford OX1 1HN
(Phone: 01865-241249; Fax: 01865-794449)

and

The David Brown Book Company
PO Box 511, Oakville, CT06779
(Phone: 860-945-9329; Fax: 860-945-9468)

and

via our website
www.oxbowbooks.com

Printed in Great Britain at
The Short Run Press
Exeter

Contents

Foreword

THE MANY READERS of English fiction who like detective stories, old or new, could probably be divided into those who regard Sherlock Holmes as the unchallenged summit of the genre and Sir Arthur Conan Doyle as the greatest-ever exponent of the deductive approach, and those who cannot stand either Holmes or his creator. I belong to the first category. When young and unemployed I memorised virtually all of the Sherlock Holmes long and short stories known collectively to their devotees as "The Canon", like those early Egyptian monks who (we are told) could daily recite the entire Book of Psalms in Greek or Coptic. The study offered here is, mostly, yet another exercise in deduction. It has been couched in Sherlockian mode because, I have persuaded myself, that may make it more readable and surely more intriguing than it would have been in the conventional format; a long and a possibly yawn-inducing article in one of the specialist journals devoted to Celtic studies, its text bristling with unfamiliar and unexplained terms and every new suggestion propped up from below by a phalanx of nervous footnotes. Academic purists will however please accept that the necessary references are given at the end, that the subject-matter is entirely serious and that, collectively, the conclusions cannot simply be dismissed because – in one squeamish reader's words – "they leave an unpleasant taste" or attribute "such a destructive obituary" to someone presented later as an ageing Christian bishop. At bottom, what follows is a research report and not a commentary on any one human's behaviour. Linguists and (especially) arithmeticians will also please excuse the several explanatory forays aimed at general readers, or at those who are puzzled by the relevance of a number-sequence like 4.9.13.22.35.57. I have at least included illustrations.

The subject is an inscription carved or incised on a stone slab in an Anglesey church. The inscription, which is in Latin and has only forty-eight letters, some of them peculiar, can here be called 970 *Catamanus* for short. The stone slab is visible, and visitable too if you can get the key of the church, but in a national context is far less accessible and consequently far less known than anything in, say, the National Museum of Wales at Cardiff. 970 *Catamanus* has appeared in guidebooks and in a good few archaeological publications, where it can be described with relative accuracy but tends then to be discussed in extremely loose manner. All the descriptions that I have read are incomplete because they fail to address the question of the slab's original nature and function. All the discussions of the inscription are defective and most of them are wrong. We are going to meet someone with a good claim to have been the first-known successful practical joker in British history.

Wales, like my native Cornwall, is a part of Britain but is distinct from England. Wales has its own Assembly now and, more importantly, its own early history within which there have been events, periods and dynasties sometimes seen as marking an Heroic Age. I apologise, but not very seriously, to any Welsh friends and colleagues who may consider that the House of Gwynedd is slighted in these pages. A detective's job is to observe, to deduce, to reach conclusions and to expound reasons for them, and only then – if ever – to moralise, ideally over a choice cold supper at 221b Baker Street. This slab, 970 *Catamanus*, can lead us far afield and can introduce us to things that should reduce that tired old expression "the Dark Ages" to its terminal obsolescence. All that is required is your close attention.

C.T.

Lambessow, Truro, Cornwall
January 2002

Acknowledgements and Conventions

IN EARLY 1997, first alerted to the concealed aspects of the inscription by seeing what happens when its forty-eight letters are restored to four 12-letter rows, I circulated ideas as a worknote to selected colleagues. Some replied understandably with ribald comments, some sent helpful suggestions or corrections, and most seemed to believe that 970 *Catamanus* is more intricate than it might appear to be. A compressed treatment of the stone was included in my book *Christian Celts. Messages and Images* (Tempus, 1998, pp. 162–8), but only as part of a demonstration of the ingenuities within Biblical-style composition attained in Wales by the 7th century. Much that is set out here had not by then been discovered. Very special thanks go to David Howlett, for his constant encouragement and help at all times, and also for being the first to observe – in so unexpected a source – the motif of letters behaving improperly. His find sent me back with delight to a far older Latin writing that, as a schoolboy, I had been sternly discouraged from reading. Contained in the present essay are all the features required to understand the inscription, its strata of messages, its status (we hope, unique) among early Cambro-Latin memorials and as much as can be deduced about its enigmatic composer. At the end, along with suggestions for *Further Reading* in this field, the *References* take up the academic slack. Readers who simply want a good story from early North Wales can ignore them.

Diagrams that involve no more than rows of capital letters arranged in rectangles or squares, sometimes with lines drawn around certain letters, are treated as part of the text. All the proper illustrations – maps, lettering as it appears on the actual stone and various other pictures – have been numbered as Figs. 1 to 14. In them, any drawing reproduced wholly or partly from *The Early Christian Monuments of Wales* is shown by courtesy of the National Museum of Wales, whose pre-1950 draughtspersons made them for V. E. Nash-Williams. Similarly anything taken from R. A. S. Macalister's *Corpus Inscriptionum Insularum Celticarum* is with acknowledgements and thanks to the Controller, Stationery Office, Dublin. Two drawings, in Figs. 2 and 7, are taken by kind permission from the Royal Commission on the Ancient and Historical Monuments of Wales 1936 *Anglesey* volume, and remain Crown Copyright.

Conventions have been kept to a minimum. A few special usages of Biblical style like 9:13 → 22, and Δ 10, are explained in the text. Phonetic equivalents, representations in print of past or present speech, are placed between slashes as /kadvan/, as far as possible avoiding the usual range of phonetic symbols. An asterisk or star, as in "*mandu-*", denotes a word or name not necessarily attested in any surviving writing but agreed to be safely inferred from what is known of historical linguistics. Square brackets [ ] have two uses. In citing inscriptions, usually Latin ones, they enclose letters and words that are now illegible through physical damage but can plausibly be supplied, as [G]VIRNIN. For translations, or passages in English, they denote words not originally included, but which should be added to make clear the sense, as "[the stone] of Eternus".

Finally, for the *References* at the end, while many have to indicate matters found only in learned journals and obscure works, an effort has been made to choose for preference sources like the Penguin Classics, or books likely to be found in public libraries.

List of Figures
(other than lettered diagrams in the text)

Part One

Llangadwaladr and the Catamanus Stone

The site and the monument

LLANGADWALADR is a small parish on the south-west coast of Anglesey. Its parish church, originally dating from around 1200, has been largely rebuilt in modern times.[1] Within the church, built into the inner north wall of the nave, there is an inscribed stone slab,[2] roughly rectangular; it now measures about 4 feet, 123 cms, across and 20 inches, 51 cms, vertically, its longer axis being horizontal. On the left can be seen a long-stemmed cross, the upper three arms being expanded or splayed, viewed on its side. Most of the surface is occupied by five, or more correctly four-and-a-bit, lines of letters. Some are of unfamiliar appearance and most are of uneven size.

In the 19th century and earlier, the slab formed the lintel over the south doorway of the nave.[3] Older depictions shown here as Fig. 1 – *left*, in

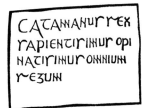

Fig. 1: The Llangadwaladr inscribed stone, partly obscured when in use as a lintel: left, from Gibson's 1722 edition of Camden's Britannia, right, from Petrie's drawing in Westwood's Lapidarium Walliae.

Edmund Gibson's 1722 edition of Camden's *Britannia*[4], *right*, J. O.
Westwood's reproduction in his *Lapidarium Walliae*, 1876–79, of a drawing
by G. Petrie – omit the long-stemmed cross. This must be because, when
serving as a lintel, parts of the slab to left and right of the actual inscription
were concealed within the masonry of the south wall. Fig. 2 gives the two
best representations. The upper drawing was made before 1937 for
RCAHM Wales *Anglesey* inventory[5] and the lower, probably drawn from
photographs, for *ECMW* in 1950.[6] It has to be pointed out that it is
extremely difficult to photograph this inscription for various technical
reasons, but that the two displays in Fig. 2 suffice for present purposes.

   Here and throughout this book, when any inscription is mentioned, we
can follow an established practice of printing them in CAPITAL
LETTERS even when, as here, the letters are strictly book-hand or
"lower case", and also of putting a slash / to mark the divisions between

*Fig. 2: The inscription as visible today: above, drawn for the 1937 Anglesey RCAHM
Wales volume (Crown Copyright), below, probably drawn from photographs, for The
Early Christian Monuments of Wales, 1950.*

lines of lettering. The Llangadwaladr stone is still quite legible and relatively well-preserved. As an inscription it has two reference-numbers; 970, the one preferred, in *CIIC*, and 13 in *ECMW*.[7]

The lines can be made out as:

CATAMANUS / REXSAPIENTISI / MUSOPINATISIM / USOMNIUMREG / UM

– and readers are invited to check this transcript with Fig.2. Sorting it out, we find six words, a Celtic (British) male personal name and then five words in Latin. With slight rearrangement we now have:

CATAMANUS . REX . SAPIENTISIMUS . OPINATISIMUS . OMNIUM . REGUM

– which, as a word-for-word translation, signifies:

"Catamanus . king . wisest . most-renowned . of-all . kings"

Problems

But this is a point, and it falls almost at the beginning of our study, where genuine uncertainties pop up. Immediately they must involve the real purpose, the connotation, of the six-word message or text, and then the intended function, the original physical disposition, of the parent slab. To state that 970 *Catamanus* was and is the tombstone of a king so-named is to ignore any number of contrary indications.

There are hundreds of such stones, as flat slabs, as natural or shaped pillars, even as boulders, scattered across both Ireland and Atlantic Britain from south-west Scotland down to Cornwall, bearing inscriptions in several scripts and alphabets and mostly dated, insofar as they can be dated at all closely, between the 5th and 8th centuries AD. The inscriptions are usually short. They exhibit personal names that can be Celtic (British and Irish) or less often perpetuate Roman names current in Roman Britain and Gaul. These go with texts that are virtually all in Latin. Many of the latter are repetitive or formulaic, using brief phrases that can be linked to Christianity; HIC IACET or HIC IACIT "here he-or-she lies", with elaborations like HIC IN TUMULO IACIT "here in the grave he-or-she lies". In some instances we have older reports that apparently link such inscribed stones directly with graves and burials. These are rare because, as indeed at Llangadwaladr, most of the stones have been moved around from place to place over many centuries, in Wales and Cornwall often to become eventually incorporated in church structures.

Nonetheless, except where there happen to be strong reasons to think otherwise, these early inscribed stones in general have long been seen as the Christian post-Roman counterparts of our modern, churchyard, tombstones and memorials commemorating individuals if not also families. One can even match aspects of the ancient and modern funerary language.[8]

It has been widely supposed that 970 *Catamanus* was a plain memorial, a lettered tombstone for a named ruler – Christian, because the slab shows a cross – designed and cut following his demise and then placed on, or over, or possibly somehow alongside, his customary burial. In fact beyond its admitted similarity to the general run of such lettered stones there is nothing that directly supports the idea. There are no words about death, or the grave. Nothing says "Here he lies". Almost as common as HIC IACIT in early Wales was the citation of a dead person's father's name, especially for the higher social grades. A stone from Caernarfonshire, 389 *Iovenali*, can be read as IOVENALI FILI / ETERNI HIC IACET, two lines, probably 6th century. It shows two of these "continuing-Roman" male names; " [The stone] of-Juvenal, of-the-son of-Eternus; here he lies". The man is qualified or distinguished by the name of his father. The name of Catamanus's father was, in Old Welsh, Iago, a borrowing of the Old Testament *Iacob*, "Jacob". On a conventional memorial we might have expected to find CATAMANUS FILIUS IACOBI, or CATAMANI FILI IACOBI, which is how it would have been inscribed.

Then there is the matter of what the text really says, if we are to translate it; how the wording is to be understood, given the very flexible word-order of Latin. Were early readers meant to divide it up as

"Catamanus – a king most wise; most renowned of all kings"

or as

"King Catamanus – wisest, most renowned, of all kings"?

And do such quibbles matter? As will appear later, probably not, but taken with the absence of any direct funerary allusion in the text they must reinforce a suspicion that this may not be an ordinary, time-of-burial, individual tombstone. Looking back at Fig.1, it can be pointed out that if the slab lacked its long-stemmed cross and if it had never been located within this ancient church at Llangadwaladr a perfectly good case could have been made for regarding it as a commemorative tablet. It might have been presented as a latter-day imitation of a Roman "building-stone"; that is, a somewhat boastful lettered slab set up by Catamanus himself, or on his behalf, at the entrance to his principal residence.

The man commemorated

"Catamanus" is at least identifiable; real, historical. He was a king of Gwynedd, ancient *Venedotia* if Latinised, a native realm covering north-west Wales with a royal seat or focus on Anglesey; at Aberffraw, quite near Llangadwaladr (see map, Fig. 3). That is agreed, as would be a claim that

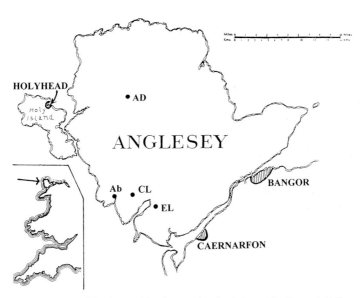

Fig. 3: Location map of Anglesey with relevant sites (scale bar, 10 miles or 16 kilometres). AD = 325 Audiva, Capel Bronwen. Ab = Aberffraw. CL = 970 Catamanus, Llangadwaladr. EL = 971 erexit hunc lapidem, Llangaffo. Modern towns are included for guidance.

he died some time in the 7th century. If written on any other medium but stone, say parchment, his name could have appeared in 7th–8th century Archaic Old Welsh as *Catuan*; a few centuries later as *Catuan* or *Catman*; and subsequently in Middle Welsh as *Cadfan*, which is how we can refer to him from now onwards. All the spellings imply much the same pronunciation, as /kad-van/. On the stone however the name is not shown as it would have been spoken in 7th-century Anglesey – /kad-ṽan/, with a very nasal /v/, indicated phonetically as /ṽ/. It has four syllables, not two, and follows a strange convention or system known as "Inscriptional Old Celtic", a kind of deliberate archaism.[9] The spelling harks back to what the same name might have been, three or four centuries earlier, in the ancestral British language. This is not exactly the same as, nowadays, choosing a mock-Latin ALBERTUS for the tombstone of an "Albert". It is more like a pedantic or learned restoration of that name to its Roman-period original in Frankish, and carving ADALBERHT.

Whoever composed the Llangadwaladr inscription apparently knew enough to reconstruct *Catuan*, "Cadfan", in ancient British. What can also be pointed out is that the chosen CATAMANUS is not actually correct. The first of the two name-elements is British *catu* "battle". The second may be *mandus*, perhaps meaning "wise", or a British noun cognate with Gaulish *mandu-* "pony" (as in "chariot-pony").[10] In either case the Latinised name would have been CATUMANDUS, and as a subsequent but still early version CATUMANNUS. Certainly on the slab one would have expected CATUMANUS; not CATAMANUS with its second-vowel A. This looks like a mistake. It may have been a deliberate one (p. 78).

We saw that claim "wisest and most renowned of all kings"; splendid words, and the rulers of Gwynedd did include a number of mighty warriors and notables. Sir John Edward Lloyd, the historian of Wales, was less impressed than he might have been, first reckoning Cadfan as "among the obscurer personalities of Welsh history" and then suggesting that, because the foundation of any original church at Llangadwaladr is ascribed to Cadwaladr, Cadfan's grandson, "the inscription may not actually date from the year of the king's burial".[11] Sir John's views had nothing to do with the question of what may or may not be implied by the inscription's wording. The death and burial of Cadfan is not recorded in any early source. It has been placed at "*circa* 625" but that is a best guess, neither an argued nor a calculated date, and it will occupy us again.

Unfortunately, as a date, it has been frequently accepted not as a feature of early Welsh history but because of its potential importance in Insular epigraphy; "Insular" means British and Irish together, epigraphy is the specialised study of these inscriptions with regard to their letter-forms and wording. Nearly all these early British memorial inscriptions dating from about AD 450 to around 600 were cut in the inherited Roman *capitalis*, a monumental script like our present-day capital letters, using a 20-letter range ABCD EFGH ILMN OPQR STVX. Letters I, V and X were occasionally also used as numerals, like XIII for "thirteen" (years); letters K, Y and Z were known but hardly ever required for these stones. Persistence of *capitalis* was partly due to its currency in Roman Britain, though another important model was certainly provided by the contemporary Christian memorials of Late Antique Gaul, Atlantic France.[12]

During the later 6th century other sorts of individual letters began to appear on inscribed stones; letters taken from the varieties of Roman handwritings – cursives, wax-tablet script, uncials and half-uncials. Together we can call them "book-hands". At first they appeared on memorials, notably within Wales, mixed with the familiar capitals. When we reach inscriptions that are assumed to belong to the later 7th and 8th centuries, these are almost entirely cut in book-hands and must have resembled contemporary manuscripts. This sequence, from capitals (= early) to book-hands (= late), may have not have been subject to identical time-scales in all regions of north and west Britain but it holds good generally. The letter-forms used for 970 *Catamanus*, which have been drawn out in Fig. 4, are not capitals. Only fourteen of a possible twenty were involved, but these best described as "half-uncials", a book-hand, with the exception of the five instances of letter A, which are much closer to another form ("uncials") and were cut larger than the others. An epigraphic enthusiast, wanting to believe that Cadfan died about AD 625 and that this slab was his contemporary memorial – with an inscription that exhibits no capitals – would be tempted to give it the status of a bench-mark. 970 *Catamanus* could demonstrate that, certainly within Wales, the inscriptional transition from *capitalis* to book-hands had been completed by *circa* 625, thus offering a fairly firm "date" in a notoriously undated sequence.[13]

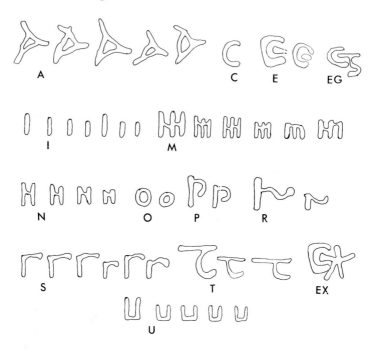

Fig. 4: The letters used in the Catamanus inscription, alphabetically sorted; only fourteen out of a possible twenty were needed. Below, right, E X is shown separately.

This could be misleading. It cannot safely be shown that the stone is Cadfan's contemporary memorial, nor can one yet dismiss an idea that the composer and designer of this text had particular reasons for preferring to use half-uncials, and large uncial A, at a period when capitals were still known and in use elsewhere. Sir John Edward Lloyd was not persuaded. Nor was Professor Kenneth Jackson, who had his own (epigraphic) reasons for proposing a date closer to "say about 650" and who also doubted "whether the Catamanus stone was actually erected on the death of Cadfan".[14]

There is, furthermore, the odd choice of the superlatives – SAPIENTISIMUS "wisest", OPINATISIMUS "most-renowned". Are they credible? Yet some have been prepared to take the inflated tone of the wording at face-value. Nash-Williams thought that "The magniloquent phraseology of the inscription plainly echoes the formal language of the

Imperial Byzantine court, which was copied by the courts of barbarian kings".[15] A subsequent writer has expanded these sentiments. "The grandiloquent phraseology has echoes of the Imperial Byzantine court and reflects the far-flung European contacts, the ambitions, and indeed the standards of elegance and learning, at the court of Gwynedd in the 7th century."[16] This claim, if singularly devoid of any hard archaeological evidence, is pretty much in step with a traditional Welsh view of Venedotia and its early kings, heroic figures of post-Roman Wales. Unhappily the second extract goes on to translate the inscription as: "King Catamanus wisest (and) most renowned of all kings (lies here)." The last two words have been invented. They were never cut.

The position, in this second year of the third millennium AD, is that capricious Fate has preserved 970 *Catamanus* in unusually good condition. It can be read, its named subject is known, the long-stemmed cross can be seen, and there is no reason to think that the slab has ever been anywhere except at the Llangadwaladr church-site. But *when* was it first planned, cut and set up here, and why? Who chose the words and composed this unique text? Why are three words so awkwardly divided between adjacent lines, and why is letter A in OPINATISIMUS twice the size of any other? Ought we to share Sir John's reserve about the sapience and renown of Cadfan? Is there really anything "Byzantine" about this six-word statement? Doubts, uncertainties and more and more questions have already started to out-number the few agreed conclusions. But in what directions should one begin to seek out answers?

The art of deduction

Sir Arthur Conan Doyle's major collections *Sherlock Holmes. The Complete Short Stories* (first so published, 1928) and *Sherlock Holmes. The Complete Long Stories* (similarly, 1929) still loom monumentally in their field, not just because they enshrine the doings of Holmes and Dr John H. Watson but because they form a dual textbook. They illustrate Holmes's deductive faculty – his baffling summaries at first glance of persons and subjects, followed by lucid explanations of how and why he made his deductions and arrived at his conclusions. From the biographies of Conan Doyle[17] it is known that Holmes's skills, as chronicled by Watson, were based on (and expanded from) the real-life medical and sociological diagnoses of Dr Joseph Bell, Conan Doyle's teacher and mentor at Edinburgh Royal Infirmary.

In the short stories Watson frequently presents himself as the necessary audience or foil. Holmes and his brother Mycroft are seated by a Diogenes Club window in Pall Mall. They are watching a passer-by ("a very small, dark fellow, with his hat pushed back and several packages under his arms"). Together they deduce rapidly that he is a recently-discharged soldier, Indian service, a non-commissioned officer in the Royal Artillery and a widower with at least two small children. Read *The Greek Interpreter* to see why and how they do this. Watson protests ("Come," said I, laughing, "this is a little too much"). Au contraire, the conclusions are inevitable and the explanations make immediate sense. As Holmes reportedly put it more than once, we *see*, but we do not *observe*.

This medium-length tale of the Catamanus stone – after we have looked at the early kings of Gwynedd, the nature of the slab as an item of Early Christian archaeology, and the character of the text – will become a detective-story. One cannot avoid some complicated passages or expositions of unfamiliar material; they accompany any multifarious Latin inscription from this distant period. Sherlock Holmes himself, despite his having written "a trifling monograph"[18] analysing 160 separate ciphers, could never have stood within Llangadwaladr church, observed the stone and its message, and then at once deduced that it was a post-mortem tribute composed by someone who knew (but could not spell out) the truth about king Cadfan; that the composer was a bishop, master of several languages, a practised cryptographer and probably Irish; and that at some stage in his life he had been to Northern Italy, visiting Geneva on the way. To reach these and associated deductions takes a good deal longer – several years – than to sum up a widowed artilleryman spotted through a Pall Mall window. The deductive techniques remain the same. Conclusions must be expounded, lucid, logical and as far as possible obvious. We shall even see that one of the simpler codes employed at 7th-century Llangadwaladr would hardly have defeated Holmes. Faced with its exact counterpart in 19th-century Baker Street, he resolved it in a couple of minutes.

———————

Anybody reading this far may want to ask, and would be justified in asking: Why should an author present an ostensibly serious, not to say academic, investigation of a famous early Welsh inscription in so uncustomary a manner? First, it ought to make for more interesting reading; as hinted earlier, accounts of old stones with weird letters and Latin words pocked out on their faces can be tedious to the point of incomprehensibility. Besides, the unpicking of the puzzles will lead us into revelations that are amusing as well as unexpected and, as late-night TV viewers are tantalisingly warned, there may be strong language and explicit images. Second, 970 *Catamanus* belongs to a minority group – about ten per cent – of all British inscriptions from post-Roman times, standing sharply apart from the main body. They are intricate compositions in a set of techniques known as "Biblical style", to be explained later. They possess arithmetical as well as verbal structures. Most contained coded elements, and some were further designed to generate "mental images" or rudimentary pictures by ascertainable rules of rearrangements. The gradual exposure, the deciphering, of an inscription with a cryptographic content demands much that could reasonably be described as detective-work, and any full chronicle of how that is carried out becomes, willy-nilly, a species of detective-story. Why not, therefore, write it as one? Third and last, by no means all who happen to see this book will know that during the last ten years or so the interest in all such inscriptions, from Britain and Ireland, has been growing enormously. They have escaped from their epigraphic pigeon-hole to the broad sunny meadows of early Insular history and Early Christian archaeology. This seems to be because of what they can tell us about survivals of learning and education from Roman Britain, of contacts with contemporary Europe, of Celtic-speaking societies and the development of the Celtic languages, of the growth of Christianity and of some remarkable, individual, intellectual achievements. Words cut in stone have a certain permanence, too. We do not apparently have undetectable forgeries among Insular inscriptions[19]. To inspect the real things, to touch them, to unravel and understand what they say, is perhaps to be as close as we can ever get to the long-gone fellow citizens responsible for these messages; composers whose names we can sometimes know. Detailed study of the inscriptions, through epigraphy, archaeology and linguistics, will always be difficult and demanding. The more painless introductions to the topic that can be provided, the better. This essay on the Catamanus stone, not too serious, not too heavy-handed, with the technicalities explained properly, has been designed as another "painless introduction", and its author's devout hope is that it can be read as one.

Life and death of king Cadfan

Pedigrees of their ruling families were of great significance among the early Welsh kingdoms. They would have been maintained, up-dated, ideally from the first committals to writing (7th century), and in some cases fictitious ancestors were inserted, most desirable being Roman emperors and grandees or even New Testament figures. A kingdom's royal genealogy was a kind of title-deed to a realm and a backbone for both biographical and narrative compositions in verse or prose. Two Welsh genealogies in particular define the royal line of Gwynedd; London, British Library, Harleian MS. 3859 (cited as Harl 3859) and Oxford, Bodleian Library, Jesus College MS. 20 (cited as JC 20). Both sources comprise "descending" pedigrees. They *descend* or go back in time, using the format "A, son of B, son of C...", putting Welsh *map* or *m.* "son" between names. Like most such genealogies they may contain partial regnal lists, or a record of successive rulers, and not invariably genuine father-to-son descents; a nephew could succeed an uncle, a brother his brother.[20] In the 9th century and probably before that, it was believed that Gwynedd's dynastic founder had been Cunedag or Cuneda, a North British potentate from Manau Guotodin (a district near modern Stirling, south-east Scotland). Cuneda had supposedly migrated, or had been persuaded to migrate, from there to northern Wales along with a bunch of sons and a grandson. If this really happened[21] it should have been around the end of the Roman period in Britain. As for the sources, Harl 3859 is a collection of genealogies carried down to the late 10th century, and JC 20 looks like a Glamorganshire compilation of the 13th century bringing together much older records.[22] The spellings of individual names reflect the absence of any single, whole-of-Wales, standard orthography or spelling-system either in Old Welsh (to around 1200) or subsequently in Middle Welsh. Copyists' errors and minor confusions resulted. Initial K-, for older C-, crept into later Old Welsh some time after 900 and vowel -w- (for short /u/ or lengthened /oo/) marks Middle Welsh. Below, headed in both cases by the Idwal, son of the Cadwaladr whose name appears in that of Llangadwaladr parish and church, names from Harl 3859 are on the *left* and from JC 20 on the *right*.

	...	Iutguaul		...	Idwal iwrch
	map	Catgualart		m.	Kadwaladyr vendigeit
	map	Catgollaun		m.	Katwallawn
**	map	Catman	**	m.	Kadwgawn
	map	Iacob		m.	Iago
	map	Beli		m.	Beli
	map	Run		m.	Run hir
	map	Mailcun		m.	Maelgwn Gwyned
	map	Catgolaun Lauhir		m.	Kadwallawn llawhir
	map	Eniaun girt		m.	Einyawn yrth
	map	Cuneda		m.	Kuneda wledic

Certain names have epithets, like *hir* "long = tall", and *llawhir* "Long-Hand = ?Generous", that need not bother us. The double-starred entries are for Cadfan, CATAMANUS. In JC 20, which might have read Kadwawn or Kadwan, a careless -g- has crept in, turning it into another name, Welsh Cadwgawn, anglicised as "Cadogan" (Earl of, etc.).

The first approximately-dated king is Mailcun or Maelgwn (both stand for a pronunciation like /mile-goon/). In a long Latin tract *De Excidio Britannie*, by Gildas, completed in or close to AD 540, king Maelgwn – there addressed by an Inscriptional Old Celtic form of his name as Maglocune – was patently a mature man, heading a group of five named British rulers.[23] Gildas also calls him *insularis Draco* "Dragon of the Isle", which suggests that there was a royal seat on Anglesey by the mid-sixth century. Maelgwn's shortcomings are specified. He was large (tall? fat? both?) as well as powerful. He had murdered a previous king of Gwynedd who was his uncle – this implies that Maelgwn was the *nephew*, not the son, of Harl 3859 Catgolaun Lauhir – but had then repented, and become a monk. Repentance was short-lived. Maelgwn put aside his wife, and next slew both her, and his own brother's son, in order to resume "marriage" with his nephew's sudden widow. "Why choose to attach to your royal neck such inescapable masses of sin, like high mountains?" wrote Gildas. More strictures followed. King Maelgwn wallowed in his crime "like a man drunk on wine pressed from the vine of the Sodomites".[24] In sum, Gildas recorded that Maelgwn's notoriety embraced, at a carnal level, marital if not sexual irregularities facilitated by the odd murder and darkened by Christian apostasy. This was Cadfan's greatest ancestor, in all likelihood genuinely his great-great-grandfather, and all of Celtic-speaking Britain knew about him; a kind of Henry VIII of post-Roman times. We may be certain that anyone knowing enough Latin to compose the 970 *Catamanus* text also knew exactly what Gildas had written.

With later names in the double genealogy, as one reaches the 7th century we are in an era of historicity, or literacy, with the likelihood of notes specifying names and years of deaths written, in ink on prepared skins, more or less at the time; and then being copied at intervals into longer records or chronicles. The death of Cadfan's father Iago or Iacob is given under 613, probably for 615, in *Annales Cambriae* as *Iacob fili Beli dormitatio* "The sleeping of Iacob son of Beli". That last word *dormitatio* "the act of sleeping" (i.e. for ever) was sometimes applied to ecclesiastics. If, therefore, Iacob had already retired to a monastery Cadfan may have succeeded his father as king of Gwynedd before this year. The death of Cadfan's son Cadwallawn, which in *Annales Cambriae* is entered under 631, in battle against the Northumbrians at *Cantscaul* (Heavenfield near Hexham), was more probably in 634 on the preferred testimony of Bede's *Historia*.[25] There is also an earlier entry in *Annales Cambriae*, under year 629, about Cadwallawn being besieged in some island (*in insula Glannauc*; this may very well be Anglesey); an entry in which he is already called *Catguollaun Regis* (*rex* = "king"). It implies that he was by then king of Gwynedd, his father Cadfan being dead.

As far as these scant historical sources go, the likely dates of Cadfan's reign are therefore from 615/613 – or perhaps a year or so earlier – to a year before 629. The proposition that Cadfan's death fell in "*circa* 625" (providing a date for 970 *Catamanus*) is seen to be drawn from the records of the demise of Cadfan's father and Cadfan's son. It may look reasonable but it is still only a guess. One might add that, on any reading, Cadfan's reign must have been short, that he could have died in this thirties, and that nothing in his vestigial history can be said to buttress a description of the man as SAPIENTISIMUS OPINATISIMUS.

Of equal interest here are Cadfan's son Cadwallawn and grandson Cadwaladr. The fame of Cadwallawn as a warrior-king, a victor in the field and a worthy Venedotian descendant of mighty Maelgwn is amply mirrored in early Welsh writings – he was much nearer the status of OPINATISIMUS than Cadfan. Cadwaladr, who became king in 634, may also have been an adolescent successor if Cadwallawn was slain in battle. There are conflicting notices for Cadwaladr's death. *Annales Cambriae* notes it under 682, linked to a *mortalitas magna*, a Great Plague, that struck Britain. One might prefer the statement in the *Historia Brittonum* of Nennius, a Welsh compilation of 829-830[26], which says that Cadwaladr "reigning among the Britons, after his father" succumbed to a plague during the reign of the Northumbrian king Oswy. But Oswy is known to have died well before 682; in 671, which might suggest that this other *mortalitas* was the pestilence of 664, noticed by Bede.[27] In any case a reign as long as from 634 to 682 would be most unusual at this time.

The date of the Catamanus stone

The place-name Llangadwaladr – the site of the church, extended to the parish and a village – prefixed that of Cadwaladr with the Old Welsh *lann* (subsequently *llan*; Cornish *lan*) that in the 7th century still basically marked "a Christian locality", further specifiable according to circumstances as "Christian burial-enclosure, the same with a church, a monastic enclosure." In medieval times, *lann/llan* took on even more meanings.[28] The significance of Llan- followed by a personal name can vary but in the case of someone like Cadwaladr, primarily remembered as a secular king and not originally as a holy man (*sanctus*) or cleric[29], a particular explanation stands out. It is that a place-name of this kind remembers a lay, or royal, founder; a man who for piety, or for the sake of his soul, gives a piece of land to the Church, causes an actual little church-structure to be built, envisages a burial-ground with special graves and in due course would expect to be entombed there himself. Sir John Edward Lloyd wondered if Cadwaladr, quitting the Venedotian royal seat at Aberffraw two miles away (see Fig. 3), had founded, if not personally joined, a new monastery here. This is arguable. Llangadwaladr had another name, Eglwys Ail, perhaps meaning "the Second Church" (Welsh *ail* "second", *cf.* Latin *alius*, originally "other" of two) as if it was a part-replacement for any court church at Aberffraw. In 1352 the vill or land-holding at Llangadwaladr was still free, and held of "Saint Cadwaladr the king", *de sancto Cadwaladr rege*.[30]

If this interpretation and idea can be entertained, it follows that an establishment bearing Cadwaladr's name should have been founded before his death in 664 – possibly around 660? – but is also likely to have been some decades later than the death of Cadfan (before 629). We edge towards a conclusion that 970 *Catamanus*, as far as is known a stone that has always been part-and-parcel of any sequence of church-structures at Llangadwaladr, cannot be taken as Cadfan's own, contemporary, tombstone. Its true date may be as late as 650 or even 660. Is it then a fresh memorial, cut at the bidding of Cadwaladr to accompany a reburial of his grandfather's remains within, or immediately next to, a new church in this new *lann*? It is a speculation, but a controlled speculation, that any reburial must imply knowledge of the original grave, that Cadfan's might have been at Aberffraw, and that if he was commemorated there at all a possible marker could have been an upright stone with something like CATUMANI FILI IACOB / HIC IACET in ordinary capitals.

Inspiration for the text?

It does not follow that Cadwaladr, even if he knew enough Latin, himself composed the epitaph for his grandfather. That task should surely have fallen to a priest, preferably of episcopal grade; a court bishop of Gwynedd resident at Aberffraw. It happens that there is a most unusual memorial stone from Capel Bronwen in Llangwyllog, a mid-Anglesey parish some ten miles from Aberffraw.[31] The inscription is a long one – thirty-five words, nearly all in capital letters with the odd half-uncial, cut in twenty horizontal lines. The likely date is some time within the sixth century. The stone is for Audiva, the wife of Bivatisus who describes himself as a *famulus Di* "slave of God", at this period, a devout professional Christian, and also as *sacerdos*, meaning "bishop" rather than just a consecrated priest. Here, using Dr David Howlett's published[32] restoration of the slightly-damaged lettering, is the "model" text of 325 *Audiva* – the original Latin composition, in full – alongside Howlett's literal translation:

AVDIVA SANCTISSIMA	Audiva, a most holy
MVLIER HIC IACIT	woman, here lies;
QVE FVIT AMATISSIMA	who was the most beloved
CONIVX BIVATISI	wife of Bivatisus –
FAMVLVS DI SACERDOS	slave of God, bishop,
ET VASSO PAVLINI	and a servant of Paulinus.
AVDO COGNATIONE	From Audus by kinship,
OMNIVM CIVIVM	of all citizens'
ADQVAE PARENTVM EXEMPLA	and relatives' patterns
MORIBVS DISCIPLINA	in morals; in discipline;
AC SAPIENTIAE	and for wisdom –
AVRO ET LAPIDIBVS	than gold and precious stones
MELIOR HEC FVIT	this woman was better.

Some of the letterings on this rough tapering stone pillar, 5 feet tall, are badly worn. On the main face, line 9, after / SOPAVLINI, has a ligature – two letters cut sharing a diagonal stroke – previously read as AN, completing line 9 with ANDOCO / and having GNATIONE starting as line 10. This was long taken, following Dr C. A. Ralegh Radford and Sir Ifor Williams, as ANDOCO GNATIONE "by race, an Andocus", despite the implausible *gnatione* (for *natione*), "Andocus" being linked to a supposed Gaulish people the Andecavi, region of modern Angers. But the ligatured AN is better read as AV "Au-", with AVDO as the abl. of a recorded male name Audus; his daughter's name, line 1, can then be restored as Audiva, with a feminine adjectival suffix, and CO/GNATIONE taken as a normal *cognatione*, abl. of *cognatio* "kinship, large family".

The long inscription is elegant and moving. Bivatisus (who has a British name) calls himself "servant, or disciple, of Paulinus", probably St Paulinus – otherwise Paul Aurelian, Pol-de-Leon – of Carmarthenshire. As a bishop (*sacerdos*) he may have chosen to bury his wife on his own estate; the stone is said to have been found in the ruins of a chapel, age unknown. The epitaph is *metrical*, thirteen lines of syllabic verse, and ends with a Biblical allusion; Proverbs, chap. 8, vv.10–11. Though FAMVLVS DI shows familiarity with some Continental epitaphs there need be nothing "Gaulish" here; the word VASSO must have been an archaism, Gaulish *uasso-*, but presumably also a British *uasso-s* because of subsequent Welsh and Cornish *gwas* "follower, disciple, servant", even "lad, boy, chap". Audiva's stone when newly cut, impressively lengthy, perhaps even heightened with paint, must have been a local feature. People would have known about it, visited it, and later remembered Bivatisus as a learned person – perhaps the first court bishop on Venedotian Anglesey, in the age of king Maelgwn.

Did king Cadwaladr see this inscription? When commissioning a memorial for his grandfather, did he have its wording in mind? Look at the common elements:

	325 *Audiva*	970 *Catamanus*
First word, name, nominative	AVDIVA	CATAMANUS
Two superlative adjectives	SANCTISSIMA	SAPIENTISIMUS
	AMATISSIMA	OPINATISIMUS
Derivatives of *sapiens* "wise"	SAPIENTIAE	SAPIENTISIMUS
"Of-all" (people)	OMNIVM CIVIVM	OMNIUM REGUM

As Sherlock Holmes might have put it, Four coincidences are three too many. No other inscription in the whole Insular series offers parallels to these two. And priority of date is not in doubt; 325 *Audiva* may be up to a century earlier than Cadfan's stone.

The production of inscriptions cut on stone

This important topic has been seldom discussed in print, and then often by scholars who might have profited from a week in a monumental mason's yard. Cutting letters, deeply and cleanly, on a stone face without spalling the surface is a hard and skilled pursuit.[33] Composing an elaborate Latin memorial, possibly with coded contents, is another skilled and time-consuming pursuit. The assumption that those who cut inscriptions like 325 *Audiva* or even the shorter 970 *Catamanus*, using what then passed for mallets or beetles and probably a set of hardened copper or bronze chisels – wrought-iron would be little use – were *also* responsible for the choice of words, selection of letter-forms and disposition of lines is ridiculous. In a few towns of Roman Britain there may have been *lapidarii*, professional monumental masons with appropriate skills and with pattern-books to show to customers, even selecting epitaphs for them (rather as happens today). None of this is remotely likely for 7th-century Anglesey.

A composition like 970 *Catamanus*, brief as it is, involved at least three stages. The author, the composer, worked out the text and its many complexities on wax tablets, or a bit of parchment, or a smooth wood slip or even a clean slate, arriving at his final version. This was the *model*, the immediate intellectual product, and its shape can often be reconstructed with complete confidence even though models as such do not appear to survive archaeologically. What was destined to be cut, to appear on a stone surface and to be necessarily larger, was the *display*. That is what we see and read, if it survives, but it was not necessarily identical with the model. The Cadfan stone has five (four-and-a-bit) lines all differing in length; its model, or certainly one version of it, had four equal lines. In real life whoever composed or commissioned a memorial inscription must have handed the cutter – who was presumably paid in kind or rewarded – a pattern to follow, a "back-of-an-envelope" miniature of the desired display. Patterns, similarly, have not been recovered by archaeology but would have been discarded anyhow.

In certain cases, and Llangadwaladr looks very much like having been one of them, the pattern for the final display could have taken another guise. The composer would transfer his pattern, full-size, on to a stone's face using some kind of paint or pigment, or perhaps powdered charcoal in grease, or by outlining all the letters with a metal point; and would then have to supervise the cutter's exact reproduction of everything. The process seems virtually certain when, as here, individual letters were required to be of specific shapes and sizes. Again, because vestiges of paint, etc., are not likely to have survived exposure over so long a time, employment of this approach can only be deduced. It is however a reasonable deduction. So is another, concerning the division of labour. No artisan could conceivably have thought out the text of the Catamanus inscription, and senior clergy do not wield mallets and chisels.

The slab as an archaeological monument

The burning question must be, Which way up? Fig. 2, earlier, shows what can be seen; a long-stemmed Latin cross (as opposed to a "Greek" cross, one with four arms of equal lengths) whose longer axis, its up-and-down, is in the same plane or direction as the axis of the lines of lettering. If the cross was displayed upright, the lines would then be vertical and any reader would have to turn his or her head 90 degrees right to make them out.

The supposition that we have a grave-stone inscribed at the time of Cadfan's death and burial implies that it might have been placed at one end, presumably the west or head end, of his east-west grave. Indeed, one guide-book claims as much:[34] "... the stone was designed to stand upright at the head of the grave, the cross vertical above the inscription, which would have been read downwards from the top right-hand corner." Behind this sweeping assumption lurks another, namely that all, or almost all, inscribed stones that can be described as tall or upright or pillar-like were set vertically in the ground, on the analogy of most of our own modern tombstones. The fact is that we have almost no direct evidence for this in post-Roman times.

The Catamanus slab is now only some 4 feet long and the top of the cross is almost at its left margin. Its thickness cannot be seen, though its former use as the nave's south-door lintel suggests that it is, and was, thick enough to be used in that load-bearing capacity. The present distance from the ends of the lines to the right-hand edge is only about one-seventh of the overall length. Practical experience tells us that, if this slab did ever stand upright, at least a quarter of its (uninscribed) length or height would have to be fixed in the ground to ensure stability.

What is the alternative? Was this slab originally something like six feet, 180 cms, long – that is, body-length – and was it meant to lie flat, as the inscribed cover or lid of a grave-cavity containing what remained of Cadfan? There are several considerations in favour of the idea. Relatively few Insular stones display a combination of Christian "art", symbolic motifs using some kind of cross, with lines of lettering. On those that do, the norm may have been a slab or pillar designed to stand vertically, but in that case its inscription is cut in short *horizontal* lines and the art is placed above the topmost line. The axis of the art is at right-angles to the axis of the lettered lines. The disposition originated in (pre-Christian) Roman personal tombstones, on which any upper pictorial elements, including little scenes in relief, dominated the multi-line horizontal inscriptions cut below.[35]

Fig. 5 shows a selection of such Insular stones where lettering is headed by art, with localities and estimated dates. The form of the cross on 970 *Catamanus* typifies a stage in its development reached by the 7th century. Comparison with Fig. 2 will emphasise the difference.

There are always exceptions and it is impossible to be certain today, but

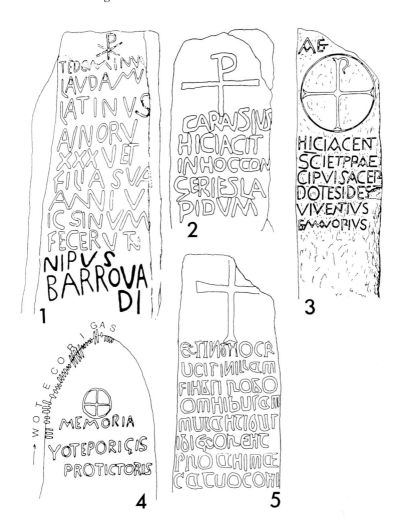

Fig. 5: Inscribed upright slabs or pillars with vertical Christian motifs above horizontal lines of lettering. 1, 520 Latinus, Whithorn, first type chi-rho; early or mid-5th century. 2, 393 Carausius, from near Penmachno, second type chi-rho; around 500. 3, 516 Viventius, Kirkmadrine, encircled second type chi-rho; early 6th century. 4, 358 Voteporigis, Castell Dwyran (with ogam), encircled equal-armed cross; mid-6th century. 5, 427 Catuoconi, Caldey Island, freestanding Latin cross; early 8th century. Nos.1 and 5 appear to commemorate the provision of Christian structures, while the other three are personal memorials. All five are compositions in Biblical style.

a tentative conclusion emerges. The Cadfan slab was never a contemporary, vertically-set, gravestone. It is likely that the medieval builders or re-builders at Llangadwaladr trimmed the stone at both ends before using it as a doorway lintel and inspection suggests that it was originally longer, even if we cannot say how long. If this is combined with an earlier suggestion, that the inscription is more likely to go with Cadwaladr's foundation of his *lann* than with his grandfather's demise thirty or forty

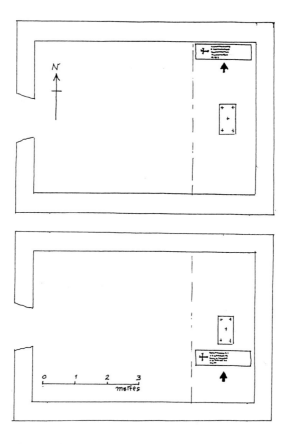

Fig. 6: Schematic ground-plans only; how the Catamanus slab might have been placed as a recumbent grave-cover within a small stone church at Llangadwaladr. Arrows show where any readers of the inscription would have stood, assuming that the Cross marked the "head" end of the grave and was consequently over its west end.

years earlier, we reach another archaeological interpretation, aided by analogies. The slab was fashioned as a long, narrow and reasonably thick stone to be placed flat, over a body-length grave lined with stones (a cist) holding Cadfan's disarticulated bones, or what survived of them in any removal from his original, pre-629, burial. This re-interment may have been inside a first small church. The fact that the inscription has survived the passage of centuries in a surprisingly legible condition suggests that for all or most of that time it was under cover, not outside in a cemetery exposed to the damp, salt-laden erosive airs of the Anglesey coast. If it was placed inside, and if both the grave and the slab as its covering lay on the east-west axis of the church itself, the cross might have been at the "head" or west end, even supposedly above Cadfan's skull; in which case the text would be read by anyone standing at the slab's southern margin. Fig. 6 gives an idea of two hypothetical placings assuming that, as with the recorded situations of other saintly re-burials within churches at this period,[36] Cadfan's last repose was at the eastern end and close to an altar. Later diversion and mundane use as a lintel-slab could imply that, perhaps by the 12th century, 970 *Catamanus* was simply a conveniently-sized stone leaning against an inner wall.

The wording, with its two superlatives

As parts of speech, the text comprises:

Latinised name, nom., subject	CATAMANUS	
Appositional noun, nom., title	REX	"king"
Two superlative adjectives	SAPIENTISIMUS	"wisest"
	OPINATISIMUS	"most-renowned"
Qualifying clause, gen.plural	OMNIUM REGUM	"of-all kings"

Previous accounts have not emphasised its oddities. It has no verb; nothing saying "he lies, he rests, he is here in the tomb". Most funerary inscriptions of this kind open with a genitive, as 386 from Llangian, Caernarvonshire, MELI MEDICI / FILI MARTINI / IACIT, literally "Of-Melus, a *medicus* (= healer); of-a-son of-Martinus; he lies [here]". In these an absent opening noun like "the tomb, the monument" seems to be implied. Again at least half-a-dozen memorials in 5th–8th century Wales

commemorate named men who, from other sources, can be identified as
local kings. Not one has a first- or second-place REX, or a genitive REGIS,
or anything else meaning "king, ruler". Adjectives are also uncommon. 402
from Flintshire reads HIC IACIT MVLI / ER BONA NOBILI, where
bona is unlikely as a feminine name and the best reading is "Here lies a good
wife (*mulier*) of Nobilis".

Only four inscriptions contain Latin superlative adjectives. Besides 970
Catamanus we have already noticed 325 *Audiva*, the wife who was both
SANCTISSIMA "most holy" and AMATISSIMA "most beloved".
Further south in Carmarthenshire is the five-line metrical epitaph,
horizontal lines across a large slab that may indeed have been a flat grave-
covering, in this case contemporary with his burial, for 360 *Paulinus* – not
St Paul Aurelian, but an important Christian layman. It reads
SERVATVR FIDAEI / PATRIEQ [ue] SEMPER / AMATOR HIC
PAVLIN / VS IACIT CVLTOR PIENTI / SIMVS AEQVI, which
David Howlett has rendered as "A lover always of Faith and Fatherland is
saved – here Paulinus lies, most pious cultivator of the just".[37]

The distinction is that in both 325 *Audiva* and 360 *Paulinus*, long
entirely Classical metrical statements of quality, superlatives are genuinely
meant. To the grieving Bivatisus his wife was "most holy, most beloved".
To the admirers of Paulinus, who had a large estate and may have founded
several churches in the area, this Christian patriot was plainly a "most
pious" figure. Nothing from early Welsh history can so far convince us that
Cadfan was really the "wisest and most renowned" of all kings (of *all* known
kings everywhere, throughout history?).

Superlatives are uncommon in Christian inscriptions from other lands.
AMATISSIMA can be matched from Mainz, Middle Rhineland, around
400 on a stone for someone's little son Bonosus ("Goody"), with its
DVLCISSIMVS ADQVE AMANTISSIMVS FILIVS "sweetest and
most beloved child".[38] The first adjective, for close-family deaths, can be
found in Spain; CONIVGI DVLCISSIMAE "sweetest wife", 5th century,
and DVLCISSIMO FILIO "for a sweetest son" on another.[39] In post-
Roman Insular Latin, as on the Continent, it was acceptable to use a single
-S- spelling when writing superlatives in *-is(s)imus*, *-a*; Mainz again, 5th
century, HIC QVIESCIT DVLCISIMVS FILIVS VICTOR "here lies-
at-rest a sweetest son, Victor". Note that *amantissimus* and *dulcissimus* are

much more than empty formulae. These memorials use intimate and touching words to express deep grief and loss.

There is one partial counterpart, perhaps, to Cadfan's text on the so-called Yarrow Stone from Selkirk in southern Scotland; 515, Yarrowkirk.[40] The eroded late 6th century inscription on a large upright slab has sixteen words in six uneven lines, all capitals. Expanding some ligatures it reads HIC MEMORIA PERPETVA / IN LOCO INSIGNISIMI PRINCI / PES NVDI / DVMNOGENI . HIC IACENT / IN TVMVLO DVO FILII / LIBERALIS; "Here, an everlasting memorial; in the grave-plot, the most distinguished Princes — [the remains] of-Nudus, of-Dumnogenus. Here they lie in the tomb, two sons of Liberalis". The memorial is an obvious instance where a composer had worked out this text, but given a pattern to a cutter who was less than literate. Lines and letters straggle, the PER ligature in PERPETVA is a mess, and -CO of LOCO was first left out and then squeezed in over LO IN.

In the 5th to 7th centuries the Britons of southern Scotland, the "Men of the North" to their Welsh compatriots, were relatively well documented.[41] They spoke Cumbric, a northern form of Late British, used Latin, were increasingly Christian, were literate, and favoured a continuing use of Roman names. There were external contacts; in 515, both MEMORIA and IN LOCO suggest distant imitations of Gaulish stones.[42] Yet no king, no pettiest of kings, with the name "Liberalis" is known. No royal sons, *principes*, with the British names *Nudoss*, *Dumnogenus*, are attested. Who were these supposedly grand folk?

Latin *insignis* "remarkable, noted, prominent, distinguished" was used sparingly, even by Cicero, and *insignissimus* is rare indeed. Did the unknown composer of this verbose, and physically isolated, memorial know enough of the structure of Latin to realise that prefix *in-* is both intensive ("very, greatly") and also negative-privative ("not")? For the second function, we have *sapiens* "wise" but *insipiens* "foolish", *utilis* "useful" but *inutilis* "useless". Suspicion grows. Can it be that, urged to produced a prolonged and flattering message for two bumpkins, sons of a Liberalis who was cock of a very local dunghill, a learned scribe obliged with INSIGNISIMI PRINCIPES but intended it ironically; "The Insignificant Princelings"? At least it offers, with its single -S- form, a parallel to the Catamanus superlatives. It might of course be wondered why, if 325 *Audiva* preferred the double -SS- spelling (AMATISSIMA), the composer of 970 *Catamanus* did not follow suit. The short answer, in anticipation, is that he needed exactly 48 letters, not 50, and could get rid of two in this manner.

A summary

Have we now deployed enough deductions, arrived at sufficient provisional conclusions, to shuffle them into a coherent scenario? Let us attempt that. Some time around 650–660 king Cadwaladr of Gwynedd, ruling at Aberffraw, had in mind his inevitable death and the desirability of arranging prayers for his soul and his salvation. Like other kings he may have flirted with the monastic life. He decided to found a *lann*, a royal burial-ground and a new church – an "Eglwys Ail", another or second church – on a royal estate not far from his seat. Mindful of his dynasty's preoccupation with the heroic past, back to the great Maelgwn and even to the founder Cuneda, Cadwaladr wanted to involve this heritage at his new foundation. Unfortunately the bones of his father the warrior-king Cadwallawn had been lost on a battlefield in distant Northumbria. Never mind; those of grandfather Cadfan, which had rested at Aberffraw since the 620s, could be located and exhumed.

Consulting his bishop, Cadwaladr learnt that in Ireland and in parts of Christian Northumbria it was now the fashion to disinter the remains of saints, indeed of a few saintly kings, and to arrange formal re-burials within churches; a custom called *translatio*. The question of a suitable inscription would have arisen. Perhaps someone remembered that, not far away, an impressive Latin epitaph for Audiva could be inspected at the estate of an earlier bishop. Probably Cadwaladr and his bishop rode over to look at it. The king, naturally, would want something on similar lines. Advised that, on the proposed new narrow tomb-cover, there would really not be space for another 33 words, he settled for the name, the word REX of course, a pair of superlatives and – as an advance on OMNIVM CIVIVM "all citizens"? – something grander, say OMNIUM REGUM.

Work would have proceeded. Cadfan's bones were exhumed, a new grave within the church was prepared, and a pattern for its cover, complete with a distinctive Cross, produced for royal approval. Under close supervision a reliable mason then cut it. The Cross, powerful symbol of the Faith, was prominent above Cadfan's skull. The king, his family and his immediate circle, some of whom would have understood what the Latin said, must have been gratified. A really appropriate epitaph for Grandfather! and, from its wording, worthy of the House of Gwynedd.

Thirteen centuries later, Victor Nash-Williams thought so too. The Cadfan stone is a stark reminder that (with sufficient low cunning) you can indeed fool most of the people for most of the time. A question lurks: Did the House of Gwynedd get *quite* the sort of memorial they had in mind? And the rest of the book, the second part, the detective-story proper, can provide the answer.

Part Two

The Inscription Analysed

A literary figure

On the surface – on the face of it, at first glance – CATAMANUS REX SAPIEN-TISIMUS OPINATISIMUS OMNIUM REGUM has six words, 22 syllables and 48 letters, with a Latin cross on the left, and anyone who knows Latin can see what it says. The likely context of its making has now been considered at length; and that is about as far as any comment or analysis has ever gone.

This is a break-point. From here on, we plunge below the surface and see 970 *Catamanus* in what amounts to another dimension. Consider first of all the following clerihew;

  a   Old King Cadfan
  b   Was an outstandingly clever man.
  b' He understood everything,
  a' Did that long-ago king.

Aren't we told as much by the word *sapientisimus*? Now observe how this jingle could be bisected, when the first two lines or "terms" marked a, b, are matched in reverse order by the last two, b', a'.

  a   Old   King Cadfan
  a' long-ago   king

– and in the middle pair, b, b', some of the individual letters are repeated;

  b   **outstandingly** **cle**ver
  b' **understood**   **every**thing

The bold letters could be separated out and shown as capitals, so;

b	OU	ST	D	Y	EVER
b'	U	ST	OD	EVER	Y

Exactly the same treatment can be given to the inscription, noting the totals of words (W) and syllables (S) in each line.

		W	S				
a	CATAMANUS REX	2	5	*rex*, noun nom.	M	NU	RE
b	SAPIENTISIMUS	1	6	superlative adj.	API	N	TISIMUS
b'	OPINATISIMUS	1	6	superlative adj.	PIN	A	TISIMUS
a'	OMNIUM REGUM	2	5	*regum*, noun gen.	MN	U	RE

Apart from the slightly-contrasted API N / PIN A, which is like Y EVER / EVER Y above, the halves of the text mirror each other. They strive for reverse symmetry. They illustrate a literary figure called "chiasmus" (adjective, *chiastic*; a, a', etc, are chiastic *terms*), or a statement followed by its re-statement or paraphrase in reverse order. For many short inscriptional texts one can recognise a chiasmus, but with not enough words it has to be padded out by matching parts of speech (noun / noun) or contrasted notions (past / future), and by using common letters whose orders may be partly reversed within terms.

Here is a twelve-word instance, also royal, also from Wales and of the same general date (*circa* 640) as Cadfan's stone. It is the epitaph for Riuallaun king of Brycheiniog and his son Ioruerth, composed by bishop Elri, which once formed the inscribed end-slab of a large double tomb at Llanlleonfel, Brecon.[43] The expanded or model text runs: IN SINDONE MUTI IORUERT RUALLAUNQUE SEPULCRIS (central cross) IUDICII ADUENTUM SPECTANT IN PACE TREMENDUM. "In the shroud, silent; Ioruerth and Riuallaun, in the graves, await in peace the awful coming of the Judgement." The cross, in the middle line of five, marks the hinge or centre of the chiasmus.

		W	S	
a	IN SINDONE MUTI	3	6	*In*; noun ablative; adjective
b	IORUERT RUALLAUNQUE	2	5	Plural subject for b'
c	SEPULCRIS	1	3	Their present predicament
c'	IUDICII	1	3	Their future predicament
b'	ADUENTUM SPECTANT	2	5	Plural verb for b
a'	IN PACE TREMENDUM	3	6	*In*; noun ablative; adjective

As for common letters, it is quite easy to pick these out;

a	ND	E	MU	
b	UE	T	UA	N
c	U	C	I	
c'	U	C	I	
b'	UE	TU		AN
a'	ENDUM			

Most Insular Latin inscriptions in Biblical style, and a few that are not, exhibit this literary compositional device; the special form shown above can be called "inscriptional chiasmus". The chiasmus was merely one of an array of ornaments incorporated, effortlessly, in Classical Latin writing. In the Christian world it appears constantly in the Vulgate, the Bible in Latin translated or modified by St Jerome and his circle in the late 4th century (and the Bible that would have been used by now at Llangadwaladr). Some of these inscriptions are also literature. The Llanlleonfel memorial, 986 *Ioruert*, is metrical, sound Latin verse, two lines of dactylic hexameters.[44] But we are not in first-century BC Rome marvelling at the elegance and mastery of Cicero's declamations, rhetoric and letters. We are in seventh-century AD North Wales, a good century on from "King" Arthur (if he ever had anything to do with this part of the world). The common language is Archaic Old Welsh, not everybody is yet Christian, the Roman occupation is long gone and forgotten and there are no shops, roads, schools, towns or money. People live in round stone huts and local kings re-occupy hillforts. This is supposed to be the Dark Ages. Who on earth would have any time for chiastic figures in metrical Latin compositions? Who would be able to read them, let alone appreciate such finesse? Our analysis plainly has a long road to travel.

The inscription's lay-out

Underlying what is displayed on Cadfan's slab must be the model, irrecoverable physically but still readily deduced, the composer's own starting-point and original text. Some people, even at the time, might have noticed that though the inscription has six words the whole thing proclaims a certain "four-ness". The Cross naturally has *four* arms, and the postulated

larger slab as a grave-lid must have had *four* corners. The chiasmus, which
is pretty obvious, has *four* terms (not six), and there are *four* words after
CATAMANUS REX. The letters add up to 48, which is *four*-squared
times three.

There might have been (mental) queries. If the chiasmus is real and
intended, why wasn't the whole text cut in four horizontal lines instead of
this clumsy four-and-a-bit lines mode (see Fig. 2) with some words
awkwardly split?[45] Come to that, why wasn't this royal memorial nicely
realised in regular lines of capitals, which were then still known and could
just as well have been used, instead of so many straggling and peculiar
book-hand letters?

We shall find later a near-certainty that the composer planned this
specific lay-out

```
C A T A M A N U S
R E X S A P I E N T I S I
M U S O P I N A T I S I M
U S O M N I U M R E G
U M
```

because he wanted each line to contain a specific number of letters, because
he wanted certain (enlarged) letters to be in the right places and because
no conjurer reveals his secrets before a performance. If he had ordered
capitals in a regular grid, not splitting any word, so;

```
C A T A M A N U S R E X
S A P I E N T I S I M U S
O P I N A T I S I M U S
O M N I U M R E G U M
```

– it would have been bound to draw attention at once to the fact that some
letters now adjoin as vertical pairs, OO AA SS, and many more as diagonal
pairs, PP II NN NN TT II SS II MM UUU and SS. So strange and
obvious a feature might have prompted, not the composer's intellectual
equals, but casual viewers – smart young members of the royal circle,
perhaps – to start asking questions they were not supposed to ask. In this
respect the four-and-a-bit irregular lines and the not very familiar letter-
forms acted as a kind of immediate disguise.

Aspects of Biblical style

"Biblical style" is a convenient name for a mode of composition, comprising both literary adjuncts – like chiasmus, and its related device parallelism – and arithmetical ones.[46] It is not confined to the Bible, or for that matter to Latin; there are Biblical-style elements in the Greek New Testament and the Hebrew Old Testament and it is possible to compose English prose and verse in this manner. However, where post-Roman Insular Latin inscriptions and other, much longer, writings that survive as manuscripts are concerned there can be little doubt that, by the end of the 5th century, the Vulgate, as the Gospels, Psalms and the first five books of the Old Testament or as the whole work, was the prime model and inspiration.

In this mode, a writer imposes order, shape, number, ratio, pattern and ornament on what would otherwise be just a sequence of words. Some devices, like acrostics and anagrams and allotting numerical values to letters, had been used in pre-Christian Roman literature (and can sometimes be detected in Roman Britain[47]).

The brief Catamanus text, if not as complicated as, say, the 986 *Ioruert* memorial, makes heavy use of arithmetical adjuncts. These, together forming the "computus" side of any inscription or longer piece of Insular Latin, take us into a fascinating but unfamiliar realm. Mental arithmetic, an ability to add and multiply rapidly in the mind, is pretty much a lost art today (think of any supermarket till) but a skill that can be readily self-taught. Biblical-style *arithmetica*, the Latin word for this, also introduces us to some simple codes and their decipherment, techniques for concealing names and information, all governed by clues and rules that are now being rediscovered.

Two devices that must be defined, now or later, are "letters-as-numbers", or LaN for short, an alphanumerical system; and the creation of, with validation by, proportional composition involving ratios – most importantly, "extreme ratio", the so-called Golden Mean or Section. For LaN, the Latin ABC used in the earlier inscriptions and current until around 900 had twenty letters; ABCD EFGH ILMN OPQR STVX. The "V", as a capital, stood for vowel /u/ long or short, and also for the semi-consonant /w/. Though K, Y and Z are found in older Latin and in the Vulgate – *kalendae, baptizatus, hysopo* – the three were conventionally excluded from the LaN system in force at the period of 970 *Catamanus* and only later admitted to convert it into a 23-letter LaN. (Letters J, W, and the absolute U-V distinction – making 26 – are medieval features.) It takes only a moment to memorise the 20-letter LaN values:

A B C D E F G H I L M N O P Q R S T V X
1 2 3 4 5 6 7 8 9 10 11 12 13 14 15 16 17 18 19 20

– and not much longer to become practised in adding up names or words in the mind, so that the LaN value of the name CATAMANUS turns out to be 3.1.18.1.11.1.12.19.17 = 83. A common function of LaN additions was to yield numbers small and large that had their own meanings, or were symbolic, in Biblical terms. One can add all consecutive letters, or the first letters (initials) only of words or of an inscription's lines, or their last letters. Other numbers arise as the totals of words, or syllables, or letters in a text. To look at a quick example, 325 *Audiva*, bishop Bivatisus's long epitaph for his beloved wife, is overwhelmingly Christian in tone. Thirty-three words in this text could suggest a reference to a pre-Vulgate tradition, derived from the Gospels, that Christ's earthly life was 33 years.[48] Audiva's holy life (she was *sanctissima*) copied her Lord's. The seventeenth word of the 33 is her father's name AUDO. The LaN value of Old Testament ADAM – Man created by God in His image – is 1.4.1.11 = 17, and AUDO and ADAM, both four letters, share A and D. In this and other ways the memorial conveys an impression that the bishop was mourning the devout daughter of a devout fellow-Christian.

It has to be admitted that there is nothing very Christian about 970 *Catamanus* but, inspected carefully in its five-line display, it could very well start to reveal certain arithmetical clues as well as the literary chiasmus to anyone familiar with Biblical style. We shall explore this later but, for the moment, there was an earlier mention of an apparent involvement with the number *four*. On the display, line 1, CATAMANUS, has *nine* letters. Lines 2 and 3 both have *thirteen* letters and line 3, the middle one, has as its first and last letters (MUSOPINATISIM) M M, or 11 plus 11 = *twenty-two*. Those numbers, 4.9.13.22, immediately suggest the start of a longer sequence or set (4.9.13.22.35.57.92...) which was known and used in the computus of other Welsh inscriptions in Biblical style to yield extreme ratio – explanations later, p. 46. And for all those, either in the 21st century or back there in the 7th, who can claim to be quick at arithmetic, please note that 4 + 9 + 13 + 22 + 35 makes 83, which is the LaN value of CATAMANUS. Is all this just another coincidence? Not a bit of it; reflect that the "correct" spelling CAT*U*MANUS, with U/V = 19, would give 101, that there is no *linguistic* reason why lines 2 and 3 have to be 13 letters long and that we shall come across so many potential "coincidences" along these lines that the word soon ceases to have any relevance.

Step 1: reverting to the model

A Biblical-style composition with hidden features would have to be roughed out in successive draughts but, unless it was designed to be cut as it stood from the final draught, behind any actual display there would be the composer's model. Since one purpose of composing in this way was to allow recovery of hidden ideas, to communicate with others familiar with Biblical style, one assumes that an immediate model was meant to be reconstructed from a display without too much difficulty.

The inscription's letter-total of 48, four twelves, the other indications of "four" and the seeming irregularity of the display prompt, as a start, rearrangement into four 12-letter lines. With this, it is immediately notable that line 1 will be CATAMANUS REX, which has twelve letters, and one can see this is possible using the nom. form – gen.CATAMANI REGIS has thirteen. Let us set this out, with line numbers and column numbers for further reference.

1	C	A	T	A	M	A	N	U	S	R	E	X
2	S	A	P	I	E	N	T	I	S	I	M	U
3	S	O	P	I	N	A	T	I	S	I	M	U
4	S	O	M	N	I	U	M	R	E	G	U	M
	1	2	3	4	5	6	7	8	9	10	11	12

Rectangular "grids" like this could be used to give short acrostics, downwards readings, but there are none here. What *can* be seen is that one result of writing single -S- superlatives is to show most of the letters as vertical pairs, or twice as triples, SSS in cols. 1 and 9, even a diagonal, col. 4 to 7, with NNNN. There are no less than nine vertical pairs. In all, at least twenty-eight letters are involved in these adjacencies; over half the total. If this is the immediate model, can its structure possibly be regarded as accidental? Surely not; but where does one go from here?

Step 2: drawing shapes

If, instead of letters, the grid consisted of the numbers 1 to 48 disposed haphazardly, to modern eyes it would resemble a puzzle from those undemanding drawing-books intended to keep small children quiet on journeys. One has to join up the numbers in the right order to make a picture of Bob the Builder, a cheerful dinosaur, even – first seen in 1999 – Tony Blair. In the 7th century anyone who read the memorial, counted its letters and memorised the wording and the exact spellings, catAmanus, sapientiSimus, opinatiSimus, could go away, find a piece of smooth slate, get out a pocket-knife and repeat the grid we have just examined as the putative model. Looking at the result, one's next step would be to scratch rectangles or oval "sausages" around the vertical pairs, triples and NNNN diagonal. This is what the grid now looks like:

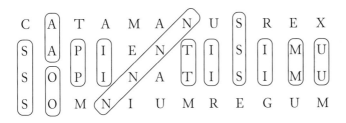

Supposing that, as argued earlier, the inscribed slab was horizontal and it was generally thought that Cadfan's skeletal remains also lay horizontally in a grave below it, an awful realisation dawns. This is all starting to look like a human figure. As the reproduction on a slate could be turned through a right-angle, we can do the same thing on paper, in print, and look at it vertically, so:

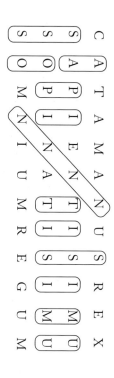

And yes! It *is* a picture of somebody, presumably king Cadfan. Any innocent sharp-eyed toddler (who should immediately be shielded from further revelations) would tell you as much. We have a Snoopy outline here, a kind of Lego-man. The cluster now at the top with SSS and OO and AA must be his head. The NNNN diagonal is obviously an arm. But what about the fourth row up, the one with E and SSS? What else *could* it be? Have we been tricked into a simulation of the long-deceased, the very dead, king Cadfan as sexually aroused?

In the 7th century and probably later the most sober and learned cleric, the most acute Latinate intellectual, who got this far must have burst into laughter, albeit mirth tinged with horror. The grotesque incongruity of what can thus be generated from a Christian memorial, the sheer audacity of doing so, induce sudden shock. To appreciate the cruel joke at its fullest one has to know Latin – as many contemporary enquirers would have done – and we come to that in a moment.

Meanwhile, still trying to look at 970 *Catamanus* through the eyes of a contemporary scholar, we turn again to the text because the apparent denigration of the dead king might be a reminder of certain words. It could be a surprise to see Cadfan described here as *sapientis(s)imus*. That particular accolade had been reserved, above all, for the sixth-century British writer Gildas whose works and personal reputation merited it. In *Annales Cambriae* his death in 570 noticed him as *Gildas Brittonum sapientissimus* "wisest of the Britons". In 793 Alcuin of York, citing something to be found in a book by Gildas, could still write *in libro Gildi Brettonum sapientissimi*. How could a not obviously distinguished king of Gwynedd lay claim to a similar title? Or was the word a clue, a pointer, to something Gildas had written?

It would have been common knowledge that Gildas, in his *De Excidio Britannie* of 540 a century before Cadfan, dwelt at length on the many negative aspects of Maelgwn, Cadfan's heroic ancestor. He alluded to Maelgwn's physical size, but distressing lack of any corresponding moral stature. "The King of all Kings" (= God) "has made you higher than almost all the generals of Britain", wrote Gildas. "Why do you not show yourself to Him better than the others in character, instead of worse?"[49] In Latin this starts "Quid te non ei *regum omnium* regi..." Whether or not the inscription's final OMNIUM REGUM was first suggested by the 325 *Audiva* OMNIVM CIVIVM, here it is, reversed, from a passage by Gildas *sapientissimus*. Is there an implication that in his own personal and sexual life Cadfan, despite the impressive epithets, had been no better than his great-great-grandfather?

Step 3; Letters into words

When visiting a royal church and examining the message on a royal tomb-slab it is unwise to utter critical or ribald remarks; dangerous, too, in an early Welsh milieu where insults, and their dire consequences, were classified like so many butterflies. The prudent visitor, having sought out a quiet corner and a bit of slate and having got as far as the Lego-man outline, would not take long to detect a further level of authentication. Let us now return the dead, but still distressingly priapic, monarch to a supine posture lying on his back on the grave and renumber the columns.

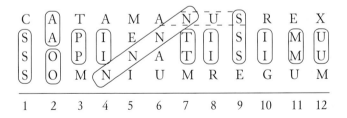

All the bits of Cadfan's body are labelled appropriately, from top to toes. The letters, single, double, or triple, are initials of Latin words that describe parts of a human body and they occur in the right order, from left (the head end) to right. All the words are ordinary. Some are singular, some plural. A body has one head, one chest, but two arms and two feet.

1. S S S   *Summae* [*partes*] "the topmost, uppermost, bits" – crown, the scalp, top of the head (and see under cols. 11–12). Allowing that single letters can be relevant within their columns, C, the first letter, must suggest *Caput* "head".

2. A A O O   These pairs, on the same level, are for *Aures* "the ears" and *Oculi* "the eyes". For anyone supine, strictly A A should be below O O. Using *sapientisimus* the composer was stuck with four A's in the first two lines; the need to find a second O may explain his choice of the obscure word *opinatisimus* to make the pair with *omnium*.

3. P P   As the lower half of the head and face, and throat, *Palatum* "palate, organ of taste" (= "mouth") is likely. Latin borrowed certain "body" words from Greek, but the Greek *pharynx* "the throat-cavity" was not among them.

4. I I   Moving downwards slightly, looking for anything in pairs, *Iugula* "the collar-bones" would be suitable.

5. N N N N   Clearly this is an arm outstretched. Latin *brachium* "the whole arm" is excluded because the text has no B. The arm ends at the top of col. 7, where the last N is appropriately middle letter in M A N U S, *manus* "hand". Do we have an action-shot? N suggests the word *Nexus* "an entwining, binding-together, grasping", used by Ovid to describe a wrestler in action.[50] Here, perhaps, it is an eager king seeking to grapple, Maelgwn-fashion, with a submissive woman. (Or, alas, a man, if one reads four of the letters as A N U S "the anus"; see n.75.)

7. T T   Though pushed downwards by NNN this should be *Thorax* "the chest, the breast", a loanword from Greek. An unattested plural *thoraces* would be meaningless.

8. I I   *Intestina*, plural, "the intestines, the guts, innards". Since it marks the stomach-area note, top of column, the correctly-placed U for *Umbilicus* "the navel".

9. S S S   There were plenty of coarse impolite words in Latin, as in English (and Welsh), but in this case the three S's – depicting length, not triplicity – allow *Sexuale* [*membrum*] "the sexual member, organ", neuter singular. Can one doubt that the E, below, is for *Erectum*?

10. I I   The position indicates *Inguen*, or perhaps its plural *Inguina* – both were used – meaning "the groin, front part of the body between the hips". Probably by chance the bottom letters in cols. 9-11 supply (i n) G U E (n).

11–12   We come to the legs, which must lie horizontally. This suggests that M U over M U, suitably paired, stands for *Membra Ulteriora* "the nether limbs, the legs", in contrast to col.1 *Summae* [*partes*]. It could be argued that col.12 U U separately, or also, marks the toes as *Ultimae* [*partes*] "the furthest, most distant, bits", but observe, tops of cols.11–12, the E X. Is this for (sticking-up) toes, as *Extremitas*, or *Extremitates*, plural – as in "The bed came untucked and my extremities were frozen"?

Is this all? Not quite; look again at the top line where the final N of *Nexus* becomes the central N of *MaNus* "a hand". What is that hand doing? With what does the -S of *Manus* so shamefully coalesce? It rests on the *Summa* "tip, point" of the *Sexuale membrum*. Is Cadfan, frozen in well-merited death, being additionally shown as engaged in a disgusting subsidiary hobby?

It is far from easy for those unfamiliar with the by-ways of Insular Celtic Latin writing and the intricacies of Biblical style to accept that such curiosities are real; planned, designed, put on display and meant to be uncovered. It seems to be hardest for scholars whose perceptions of Early Christian Britain and the nature of its inscribed Christian memorials – all memorials – are deeply entrenched. It can become almost impossible to accept the bizarre interpretation of Cadfan's inscription, which is apparently unique in its treatment of a dead king's memory but otherwise goes with some twenty inscriptions in Biblical style, some far more intricate. As we continue, the accumulation of what might individually be shrugged off as coincidences becomes too weighty to be dismissed. The analysis of this text, and its parent slab, has adhered to factual observations, supplemented by simple conclusions arising from deductions that can be explained and justified. The text has 48 letters and a cross. Arrangement into a twelve-by-four grid is hardly far-fetched. Because of the chosen words, and in some cases one can put forward likely explanations for choices, the paired and tripled letters fall as shown in the diagrams. Drawn around, the resulting picture is either sheer accident or what it looks like – a supine male human. The words denoting parts of the body, or their relative positions, from scalp to toes are constricted to those whose initials come within the 14 letters used in the text, and they are all what anyone competent in Latin would supply. The left-to-right direction is both the direction of reading, and the direction from the head downwards; the head should anyhow be on the left because that is where the Cross was. Sceptics who might agree that the diagram is rather like a Lego-man, but regard the allocation of the Latin labels as arbitrary, are welcome to propose a range of alternatives (going from right to left, say, and finding a "head" word starting with X, U or M).

Generating an image

What we have seen, a necessarily distorted picture of dead king Cadfan, is something whose origins lay in the Romans' world of letter-games; a making of patterns from words and letters that can convey ideas well outside the immediate sense of any text. Apparently in several parts of Wales and apparently at some time after AD 500 the inscriptional variety of Biblical-style composition was enriched with a capacity to generate "mental images". They can be defined as rudimentary pictures, frameworks to be fleshed out in the minds of viewers and readers, helped by the sort of initial-letter or part-word labelling that we have just examined.[51]

Mental images come in different guises. As almost all Insular inscriptions are Christian statements, the images are almost all religious or Biblical; ground-plans of the Heavenly City, of the Holy Sepulchre, of specific grave-plots, and in one case a most elaborate depiction of the Crucifixion. The image generated from 970 *Catamanus*, if one wants to classify it, is "a devised profile". It is a side-on view of a dead man lying on his back, a horizontal *profile* as opposed to anything seen from vertically above it (a *plan*). It is *devised* because, unlike a few images that are detectable at once in a display, Cadfan's required two tricks or devices to bring it into play. First, the five-line text had to be turned into a four-line rectangular grid; second, appropriate letters needed to have little ovals drawn around them. Neither device was directly indicated by the textual display.

As to why anyone should have wanted to do this, we can postpone further deductions and eventual conclusions. Because the revelation of Cadfan's imperfect life was foreshadowed by suspicions about his proclaimed stature the image was less of a shock than it might have been. There were several reasons, as we saw, to think that the wording was not meant to be taken at face-value, however well received those superlative adjectives may have been at the court of Gwynedd. And that in turn could mean that the composer envisaged, at the time, potential readers of his text who were better educated, or more aware of deeper meanings, than his royal patrons. He was operating on two levels. He may even have been operating on three or four.

There is more to come in the way of lambasting king Cadfan. The exposure of his posthumous sexual stamina, accusation of self-abuse and a general aura of moral turpitude to match the shortcomings of his great-great-grandfather together make up no more than an opening salvo. The big guns of Classical learning have yet to open fire. It is high time to meet the author. A person prepared to go to such lengths is unlikely to have refrained from "signing" his little masterpiece. If he did so for the enlightenment of future generations his name may lurk a long way below the surface. While making it possible for a minority of readers to find the immediate supine-Cadfan image – the very existence of which could be strenuously denied – intricacies of Biblical-style composition would and did allow him to conceal many other things in far less accessible form.

An auctorial name, which quite a few of these inscriptions have proved to contain, is recoverable only through the range of devices used to encode or hide it. The process has to be detected, and then reversed. It would seem that the rules of this game required an author to incorporate essential clues in his compositional structure and computus. Our man did so. We can see what they were, and how the decipherment can be accomplished.

How to hide a name

Within many short British inscriptions dating from the 4th to 11th centuries one popular method was to include a name, usually taken as the composer's or author's, as an acrostic; either by reading down letters on the left margin, a true acrostic, or the last letters on the right margin, a telestich. Acrostics, which started way back in the Roman world, have never lost their appeal. Lewis Carroll's poems are full of them.

Unless an inscription shows a number of lines with letters directly above each other it may be necessary to alter the letters into a square or rectangular grid. An example from Gwynedd, 393 *Carausius* from near Penmachno, was shown in Fig. 5. It dates from around 500. The text is CARAVSIVS

/ HIC IACIT / IN HOC CON / GERIES LA / PIDVM, *Carausius hic iacit in hoc* – *Congeries lapidum*, "C. here lies in this [grave, tomb, cairn] – A heap of stones". It has 38 letters but it seems to have been allowable to make a four-divisible total, and thus a grid, by starting again at the beginning, using an added CA-. One soon finds that the grid is eight across, five down:

C	A	R	A	V	S	I	V
S	H	I	C	I	A	C	I
T	I	N	H	O	C	C	O
N	G	E	R	I	E	S	L
A	P	I	D	V	M / C	A	

– when the telestich gives the name, VIOLA. This clever girl worked a great deal more into her epitaph for Carausius, who was her *privatus* "sweetheart".[52]

In this case, as in others, though Viola appears acrostically in a rectangular grid the first letter of her name – capital V as /w/, borrowed from the V as /u/ in Carausius – would be the eighth letter in the whole text written as a line. The reading could be linear:

Carausi **V** shiciac **I** tinhocc **O** ngeries **L** apidum/c **A** = VIOLA
    7   7   7   7   7

The letters of "Viola" are now spaced out with regular intervals having seven letters each, and if one knew this in advance, if the actual interval-lengths had somehow been advertised, the grid and telestich would not be needed.

The name for this linear presentation, something that obviously arose from acrostics, is a "precession-and-interval" reading. It can be found with many variations.

————————————

In *The "Gloria Scott"*, a short story, Sherlock Holmes is asked to examine a note that, seemingly harmless, had struck a Mr James Trevor dead with fright when he read it. "The supply of game for London is going steadily up," it said. "Head-keeper Hudson, we believe, has now been told to receive all orders for fly-paper, and for preservation of your hen-pheasant's life." Because this makes no proper sense – head-keepers ought to be bad news for hen-pheasants – Holmes deduced that it probably disguised something in code. Though Watson omits to tell us as much, Holmes would have noticed the prominent doublets, *head-keeper*, *fly-paper*, *hen-pheasant*, and worked out that this text should contain two-word blanks. It is another precession-and-interval piece using words instead of just letters, with the shape Word – (2 words) – Word – (2 words) – Word ..., reading word no.1 and then onwards every third. "The game is up. Hudson has told all. Fly for your life" was the message that finished old Trevor, a man with a black past. An alternative coding could have started with an interval, like the linear reading of VIOLA, and then have used three-word intervals. With this, "The game is up" could be encoded as "In high summer, *the* cricket season, the *game* rules all; it *is* now steadily going *up* in popularity everywhere". And a suitable clue or pointer here might be a little drawing, showing three stumps of a wicket.

Greater concealment is possible when any such intervals, instead of being equal or regular, 7.7.7, 2.2.2 or 3.3.3, are irregular and incremental. Intervals might be drawn, say, from a sequence like 1.2.3.5.8.13.21.34.55, which begins the first Fibonacci number set (see p. 46), or from a geometric progression like 2.4.8.16.32. When this happened, it was necessary to build into the computus of an inscription various arithmetical clues, for the sake of readers; one or more of such clues helped to identify the values of intervals. At least six early inscriptions from Wales composed in Biblical style contain precession-and-interval readings, mostly of authors' names, that have incremental or irregular intervals. These codes can be solved but not very easily, nor by beginners.

Here is a modern illustration containing the name "Nancy", using 1.2.3.5.8.13 as the intervals, and starting a reading on the second letter. The matrix text is the bland advice "In planning new schemes, stay cheery and bold" and the reading goes thus:

i **N** pl **A** nni **N** gnews **C** hemessta **Y** cheeryandbold = NANCY
1   2   3   5   8   13

In another variant a sequence of incremental numbers acts, not as intervals, but as *indicators*. They indicate the required letters, counting the latter from no.1 onwards. The name "Fred" has four letters and an appropriate sequence would be a doubling-up each time from 4, as 4.8.16.32. The matrix is "The fine red pen prepares a secret word."

The	Fine	Red	pen	prEpares	a	secret worD	=	FRED
	4	8		16		32		

Precession-and-interval readings on these lines survived throughout the Middle Ages; recommended in textbooks on cryptography, they can be applied to texts in almost any language, much longer than those of Insular Latin inscriptions. The medievalist M. R. James introduced one into what must be among the creepiest of his ghost stories, *The Treasure of Abbot Thomas*.[53] An English chapel has three stained-glass windows brought from the German abbatial church at Steinfeld. They depict Job, John the Evangelist and the prophet Zachariah. Around the borders of their robes are jumbled capital letters, 38 on each. Mr Sanderson, an antiquary, is intrigued and begins by noting down the three groups of letters:

Job   DREVICIOPEDMOOMSMVIVLISLCAVIBASBATAOVT
John   RDIIEAMRLESIPVSPODSEEIRSETTAAESGIAVNNR
Zachariah   FTEEAILNQDPVAIVMTLEEATTOHIOONVMCAAT.H.Q.E

"I realised almost at once that I was dealing with a cipher or cryptogram" Sanderson later explained to friends, "and I reflected that it was likely to be of a pretty simple kind, considering its early date." Simple or not, he soon realised it was a precession-and-interval reading ("After the first letter you skip *one* letter, after the next you skip *two*, and after that skip *three*" – and so on), giving him intelligible Latin:

DECEMMILLIAAURIREPOSITASUNTINPUTEOINAT...

but leaving the rest buried in all the omitted letters. He then found that one was expected to read every *alternate* letter, giving;

RIODOMUSABBATIALISDESTEINFELDAMETHOMAQUIPOSUI-
CUSTODEMSUPEREA

and ending, not with Latin but French, GAREAQUILATOUCHE. So the whole message was *Decem millia auri reposita sunt in puteo in atrio domus abbatialis de Steinfeld a me, Thoma, qui posui custodem super ea. Gare à qui la touche* ("Ten thousand pieces of gold are laid up in the well in the courtyard of the Abbot's house at Steinfeld, by me, Thomas, who have set a guardian over them. Ware to him who touches it"). Mr Sanderson went to Steinfeld, climbed down the well and found rather more than Abbot Thomas's treasure. The rest of M. R. James's tale can be imagined.

How did he break the code? For the second part, knowing that *in puteo in at-* ought to continue as *atrio* and then seeing that he was left with letters commencing RVIIOPDOO..., or **R** v **I** i **O**, to take alternate ones was obvious. For the first part, the repeated 1-2-3 intervals, we are back to "hen-pheasant" or three cricket stumps. On the stained-glass windows the antiquary had carefully noted that Job had *one* forefinger extended, John blessed a book with *two* fingers and Zachariah had *three* fingers pointing up. The lesson is that anyone creating a coded precession-and-interval reading, ancient or modern, cut on stone or offered as fiction, who expects it to be resolved must supply arithmetical clues. They are essential. Without them, a trial and error approach could continue indefinitely. As Mr Sanderson explained, "I read over my notes, hoping almost against hope that the Abbot might himself have somewhere supplied the key I wanted." One could write very much the same in relation to Cadfan's memorial and others of its kind; happily, with hopes fulfilled.

A short mathematical excursion

This will not be too alarming or challenging, but is inevitable if we are to understand the computus of the Cadfan inscription, the system inherited or evolved by these early Insular intellectuals to construct and to validate their coded words and names and the quite simple basis of composition using ratio that underlay it all.

So far the arithmetic has dealt with addition of word and letter totals, and the LaN alphanumerical values; the kind of thing one would associate with primary education, as most probably it still was at selected venues in post-Roman western Britain. A vital element in all Biblical-style composition was the use of ratios or proportions. It helps to picture this in terms of basic geometry, which is how it was first worked out by the

Greek philosophers whose writings were the foundation of Roman mathematics.

The sides of a square have the same length and two adjacent sides are equal, have a ratio of 1 to 1 – symmetry, 1:1 or "mean ratio". A double-square rectangle has adjacent sides in a ratio of 1 to 2 or 2 to 1, "duple ratio", and other elementary ratios are 1:3, triple ratio, and 2:3, or 1:1½, called "sesquialter ratio". But there is a particular proportion or relationship, first generated by geometry, inherited from the Greek and Roman world and still known and used by, e.g., most architects. This is 1 to 1.61803..., or else (the same) .38197... to .61803, often rounded-off to .382:.618. It is called "extreme ratio", and many other names – the Golden Section, Golden Mean, Divine Proportions, ideal proportions, etc. Draw a rectangle whose sides are, say, 100 mm and 162 mm and you are looking at a shape that has for aeons been regarded as aesthetically more pleasing, closer to God as the originator of Number itself, than any other sort of rectangle.

To compose using extreme ratio means constructing a text so that its total of words or letters (or both) has an intentional break at a point dividing that total as .382 to .618; its "extreme section". For us today, extreme section of a number like 87 (words) or 318 (letters) is found at once by calculator-multiplying the number by .382 and .618 and rounding off to the nearest whole figure. In Roman and post-Roman Britain there had to be another way, which must have involved choosing in advance the required compositional total and collating other aspects of a text with it – hence our reasonable deduction that a model behind a displayed inscription might have gone through several stages. In the so-called Fibonacci number set[54] each number from the third onward (to infinity?) is the sum of the two preceding; thus, 0.1.1.2.3.5.8.13.21.34.55.89.144... The component numbers are in extreme ratio within their sum; 5 + 8 = 13, 13 + 21 = 34. This can be shown for convenience as 5:8 → 13, 13:21 → 34. The larger the numbers, the closer the ratio falls to .382:.618. We find that the fraction 55/144 is .38194 (rounded to .382) and that 89/144 is .618055 (rounded to .618).

Use was most certainly made of other Fibonacci-type sets like 1.3.4.7.11.18.29..., 1.4.5.9.14.23.37..., up to 1.12.13.25.38.63, and it is likely that all these were memorised as part of *arithmetica* within the Roman system of schooling; much as modern schoolchildren are or were obliged to memorise all those multiplication tables. We also encounter, frequently within inscriptional computus, two rather different sequences or "conventions" that do not start with 1.2.3.5, 1.3.4.7, and so on, but which progressively give extreme ratio as the numbers become higher. The first and apparently most popular is 5.7.12.19.31.50, which when doubled produces the extreme ratio of 100; 19:31 → 50, times-2, is 38:62 → 100. The second goes 4.9.13.22.35.57... and will occupy us shortly.

As well as demonstrating Man's striving towards perfect proportions and seeking to emulate God's creation of the universe by number, these arithmetical adjuncts of Biblical style had one important function we can call "validation". For example within a given text, a given total of displayed letters, there may lurk a sub-total that forms an anagram of a name or word, and does so in the shape of a dispersed or "split" anagram which the reader is expected to spot. "Really am", eight letters, has a split anagram of the name "Mary";

R e A ll Y a M = RAYM = MARY

If the span of that anagram is placed within a longer text or passage so that the span's letter-total is in extreme ratio with the total of all the unused letters, before and after, thus:

He said, / "Really am / furious".
6 8 7

– where the span is 8, and 6 + 7 = 13, and we have 8:13 → 21 from the set 1.2.3.5.*8.13.21*.34.55..., the split anagram has plainly been validated. It can probably be taken as genuine and intended. Readings not so validated are on the whole to be rejected.

The importance of extreme-ratio validation emerges with another recent discovery. Welsh cryptographers at this period introduced the complication of backwards readings. As far as can be made out, this was an independent Insular invention. When such readings were intended their presence was signalled by either of the Latin words *rursus* and *retrorsum*, meaning "[Read these letters] backwards", built into a text as a split anagram – slightly less difficult to detect than might be thought, because *rursus* contains RR SS UU and *retrorsum* has three R's. A contemporary instance comes from the Ioruerth and Riuallaun memorial-slab at Llanlleonfel, 986 *Ioruert*, a text

that contains no less than four codings of its author's name. We start with
a clue that is commoner in longer inscriptions, the so-called "key numbers";
integers, usually anywhere between 5 and 20, that appear so frequently and
obviously in a display or first-level rearrangement, either as they stand or
as multiples, that one can regard them as having particular functions. In
986 *Ioruert* the two key numbers are *five* and *six*, the first being specially
concerned with "auctorial self-reference" or giving the composer's name.
The first *five* words are IN SINDONE MUTI IORUERT
RUALLAUNQUE, "Silent in the shroud, Ioruerth, and Riuallaun" (his
father). Because the words contain letter R three times, at least *retrorsum*
is possible. Here it is, as a much-dispersed anagram:

in / S ind O n **EMUT** i io R ue R t R / uallaunque = SOEMUTRRR
2   19   10

– and crossword-puzzle fans will at once see SOEMUTRRR =
RETRORSUM. There are 31 letters; the span has 19, letters before and
after make 12. But 12:19 → 31, from that convention 5.7.*12.19.31*.50, at
once validates this. Now, obviously, we write the letters backwards:

euqnuallaur   treuroi   itum   enodnis   ni

and suspect that the result is long enough to house a precession-and-
interval reading. The weight of key number *five* suggests a start using '5'
for regular intervals:

E   uqnua   L   laurt   R   euroi   I / tumenodnisni   =   ELRI
5   5   5   12

It provides the name of bishop Elri as that of the author. It is also validated,
because the span of the reading, (3 x 5) + 4 = 19, and the 12 letters after,
give the same extreme ratio as before, 12:19 → 31.

Back to Cadfan's stone

The Catamanus inscription does have a computus, but its existence was
very much secondary to the generation of the supine-Cadfan image and
other cruel jests yet to be described. Its purpose was to encode the
composer's name – several times, both backwards and forwards, using

precession-and-interval and validation by extreme ratio. Our starting point must be to find what numerical clues were provided. In fact they are clearly signalled in both the display and the four-line model, as transpires when one lists the significant numbers. Note that their occurrences can overlap or be connected.

4   *Four* chiastic terms; *four* lines in the regular, or model, grid; *four* syllables in CATAMANUS (whereas CATUAN /kadvan/ has two); after CATAMANUS REX *four* words, having *four*-times-*nine* letters; letter-total of 48, *four*-squared times 3; the five display line-initials C R M U U, values 3.16.11.19.19 = 68, *four*-times-17.

9   *Nine* letters in CATAMANUS, the first word; *nine* letters in the display's first line; first occurrence of letter I, value *nine*, in SAPIENTISIMUS, comes as place no. 16, or *four*-squared.

13 In the display, lines 2 and 3 each have *thirteen* letters (as do lines 4 and 5 together); longest word, SAPIENTISIMUS, has *thirteen* letters.

22 In the display, lines 1 and 2 together have *twenty-two* letters; the text contains *twenty-two* syllables; initial and last letters of the display's middle line 3 are M M, 11.11, making *twenty-two*; letter in place no. 22 is I, value *nine*.

35 In the display, lines 1, 2 and 3 offer a progression with letter-totals of 9, 13 and 13, making *thirty-five*. Letters in places nos. 4, 9 and 13 are A S S, 1.17.17, again making *thirty-five*.

One could add, for good measure, the next number:

57 In the chiasmus, initial and last letters of "term a", CATAMANUS REX, C X, 3.20, make 23; of "term b", SAPIENTISIMUS, S S, 17.17, make 34; and 23 plus 34 is *fifty-seven*.

There are bound to be those, reading the above, who will object that it looks like a selective presentation, picking out only the figures and totals that happen to suit a desired or prearranged set. It is a perfectly reasonable criticism and it has to be answered. There would be little point in applying anything like the first, full, Fibonacci number sequence, (0.1) 1.2.3.5.8.13..., because the lower numbers can be found in almost any text. One might however look at the other non-Fibonacci convention 5.7.12.19.31.50..., employed in the computus of other Biblical-style inscriptions at this period and presumably known to the composer because he used it to validate some of his readings (e.g., p. 56). Can it be seen in 970 *Catamanus*?

5   Strictly the display has *five* (four-and-a-bit) lines; there are *five* words following CATAMANUS and the last word, REGUM, has *five* letters.

7   Letter in place no.7, N, has a value of *twelve.*

12   CATAMANUS REX, first line of the model, has *twelve* letters; the letter total of 48 is *twelve*-times-4.

After this, trying to find 19 or 31 or 50, the search tends to peter out. If we return to the evidence for references to the sequence 4.9.13.22.35.57, however, it can be emphasised that the bulk of it is derived from immediate observation – that is, from what anybody looking at the slab, displayed in any manner, would be able to see and at the same time to count. There may be a two-letters fifth line with UM but, as a general impression, this is a *four*-line arrangement with an untidy appendage, matching the *four*-armed Cross beside the text. The 48 letters are *there*; recitation out loud reveals the four-term chiasmus (and the twenty-two syllables). The totals of letters in the displayed lines are *there*. The 13-letter length of SAPIENTISIMUS, the composer's choice, is *there*. Progressing from basic mental addition to various LaN values, a system that many people then – as now, if they try – can operate mentally with extreme rapidity, the immediate totals are *there*.

The present writer's conclusion, so argued, is that the structure of 970 *Catamanus* conveys no other number-set on this repetitive and indeed obvious scale. What we are meant to detect is the sequence 4.9.13.22.35.57. And there is a clever in-built check, something that again one supposes that the composer knew. The first four numbers in the set, 4.9.13.22, add up to 48, the total of all letters. If you then add the next number 35 to 48, the answer is 83. If you pick out the letter-divisions in the 48 letters written in line, at 4/5, 9/10, 13/14 and 22/23, you have eight letters, A/M, S/R, S/A and I/M – try this as a check – whose LaN values *also* come to 83. But 83, we know, is the LaN value of CATAMANUS. None of this works with the set 5.7.12.19.

So, having been furnished with the numerical key, readers were expected to fit it into the 48-letter text and see if anything, like the composer's name, is thereby revealed. But how? One can soon realise that a precession-and-interval reading, using no more than 4.9.13.22 as intervals, would have to use up all the 48 letters just as *intervals*, leaving nothing over for any name or word. Therefore it follows that the numbers are intended to be indicators, like the 4.8.16.32 that gave FRED in the modern example shown earlier.

One could start by fitting them to the whole text, like this:

Cat **A** manu **S** rex **S** apientis **I** musopinatisi **M** usomniumregum = ASSIM
    4   9   13   22   35

The outcome "Assim" is neither a name nor a word in Old Welsh, or Old Irish or Latin – backwards, it gives *missa*, Latin for "the Mass", but surely this is accidental. (Anyone still hankering after the sequence 5.7.12.19.31 will find that its result would be MNXTT.) In all such investigation there is bound to be a certain amount of trial-and-error. Accordingly, we have to try a different approach.

Any much earlier would-be decoder, having already gaped and sniggered at the generated image of king Cadfan on his back, might well reason that the composer's opinion of the dead ruler disinclined him to have any letters of his own name mixed up with CATAMANUS REX. Removing those words leaves thirty-six letters, sufficient to hold indicated numbers up to 35. We try again:

sap **I** enti **S** imu **S** opinatis **I** musomniumreg **U** m = ISSIU
  4   9   13   22   35

And this is a known name "Issiu", attested elsewhere in Old Welsh as we shall see shortly.

Is this use of a shortened text justified? The question opens another little door. Thirty-six is a most interesting number. Apart from being the product of two square numbers 4 and 9, it is also a "triangular" number. It is the sum of 1 + 2 + 3 + 4 + 5 + 6 + 7 + 8, otherwise "the triangular number from 8", abbreviated as Δ 8. The first ten or so triangulars, 3 6 10 15 21 28 36 45 55 (55 is Δ 10), make up something else that Roman schoolchildren would have memorised. As a Biblical-style adjunct, any group of letters whose total is a triangular can be written out as an actual triangle, like a pyramid, because LaN addition of letters up the sloping sides, or along the base, or of the three "apical" letters at the angles, could be made to produce meaningful new totals. This sounds extremely difficult but could be effected by, say, changing word-order or selecting words to give letters with desired values. Here is the "triangularisation" of the thirty-six letters with the LaN values up the sides:

17	S	17
1	A P	14
9	I E N	12
18	T I S I	9
11	M U S O P	14
9	I N A T I S	17
9	I M U S O M N	12
9	I U M R E G U M	11
83	**(97)**	**106**

The *left*-side total, 83, is both the sum of 4 + 9 + 13 + 22 + 35 and the LaN value of the name "Catamanus". Does that fact in its own way validate selection of 36 letters, not 48, for precession-and-interval application and the resulting name "Issiu", or is it pure chance? Readers can try to decide. Before doing so, they might take into account, first that in extremely skilled hands any such triangularisation can be constructed to produce a relevant number – writing the two superlatives with single -S- may be one factor – and second, that triangularisation can be as inverted triangles as well as pyramids. Here is the inverted form:

	(85)	
17	S A P I E N T I	9
17	S I M U S O P	14
9	I N A T I S	17
9	I M U S O	13
11	M N I U	19
11	M R E	5
7	G U	19
11	M	11
92		**107**

Here the *left*-side total, 92, takes us back to the key sequence at once because, after 4.9.13.22, the next two numbers are 35 and 57; their sum is 92. The LaN value of the name so far discovered, as I S S I U, 9.17.17.9.19, is 71. From the inverted triangle, add all three sides – 92 + 85 + 107 – to get 284. But 284 is four-times-71. With this dual triangularisation we get, once again, no less than four coincidences linked to "Catamanus", "Issiu" and 4.9.13.22.35.57. Is it really unreasonable to accept the outcome as a Green Light?[56]

Because the inscription contains letter R only twice there cannot be a *retrorsum* anagram, indicating a backwards reading, but there could be one of *rursus*; whose dispersed span would have to stretch from the first R to the second. It would look like this:

catamanus / **R** exsapientisim **US** opinatisim **US** omnium **R** / egum = RUSUSR
 9   (13)   35   4

It seems to be validated after its own fashion, not by extreme ratio but by reference to the key sequence; unused letters, 4 and 9, the longest interval, 13, letters flanking the span S and E, 17.5 = 22, the span itself, 35.

When we write the text – the whole text, 48 letters – backwards, it looks like this. Again it seems likely that the name will avoid (reversed) CATAMANUS REX, and if it repeats "Issiu" it must begin with the first occurrence of letter I:

mugermu / **I** nmo **S** umi **S** itan **I** pos **U** / misitneipasxersunamatac = ISSIU
 7   18   23

This is not a full precession-and-interval reading – note, nonetheless, that the *intervals* in the span add to 13 – but as a whole it is acceptable because it is validated in the usual way. The span has 18 letters. The unused letters amount to 7 + 23 = 30 in the total of 48. If the outcome $18:30 \to 48$ is divided by six, and reduction from multiples was a common practice, we have $3:5 \to 8$, from the first Fibonacci set 1.2.*3.5.8*.13.21.34... Extreme ratio is shown.

There have so far been two readings of ISSIU. There may be more, including yet another backwards version. For precession-and-interval, too, we have not yet seen anything using regular, equal, intervals. The inscription is probably too short to possess clearly-signalled key numbers, but no use has yet been made of a low whole number that does seem to be mathematically prominent; seven. From the 20-letter alphabet 970 *Catamanus* used only 14, twice-*seven*, letters. Its first and last letters overall are C(atamanus) and (regu)M, C M, 3.11 = 14, twice-*seven* again. The commonest letter is I, and it occurs *seven* times. Six words and 22 syllables make 28, *seven*-times-four; and twenty-two syllables plus 48 letters make 70, *seven*-times-ten. Is this number a candidate? The forward version from the whole text is:

cataman **U** srexsap **I** entisim **U** sopinat **I** simusom **N** iumregu **M** = UIUINM
        7   7   7   7   7   7

– which is another nonsense, neither a word nor a name.

For a backwards attempt, notice that the first I, as the initial of "Issiu", would have to be letter no.8, with seven preceding it. This certainly encourages a trial;

mugermu **I** nmosumi **S** itanipo **S** umisitne **I** pasxers **U** namatac = ISSIU
        7   7   7   8   7   7

An impression that this, if it cannot be dismissed out of hand, stands as a subsidiary reading arises; first, because one of the intervals has to be 8, not 7 – "Issiu", five letters, plus six 7-letter intervals (= 42), makes only 47 and the total must be 48 – and second perhaps, because the reading runs on into reversed CATAMANUS REX. Nonetheless, it succeeds in giving the same name a third time.

Its composer's name considered

"Issiu" may look more like a phoneticised sneeze than a genuine personal name from the British past, but genuine it is. In the Book of Llandaff, *Liber Landavensis*, there is a list of church properties in south-east Wales at the time of bishop Herewald, 1056–1103.[57] Most names begin with Lann-, but there is also "Merthir Issiu". The first word is Welsh *merthir*, later *merthyr*, from Latin *martyrium*, in a special sense of "church-site possessing the physical remains of [name]". The church in question, a remote and beautiful little spot in the Brecon hills, is today Patrishow – 16th century *Patryssowe* – and its patron, of whom nothing is known, appears as "Issui".[58] There is no suggestion that it is the Anglesey composer; the site is a long way south and the foundation may be later than 970 *Catamanus*. What the church's name confirms is that this personal name could be repeated elsewhere in Wales. Its source and meaning are uncertain. It may originally have been Irish, an idea taken up later here. In the Irish 9th-century Tripartite Life of St Patrick, the names of Patrick's associates include *trí cerdda* "three craftsmen" called Essiu, Biti and Tasach.[59]

The author's status

Some, possibly most, of the people who composed these Insular inscriptions will have been priests; a group most likely to have been schooled in Latin, intimate with the Vulgate and capable of (e.g.) restoring native names to Inscriptional Old Celtic (p. 6 earlier). Two Welsh inscriptions with encoded auctorial names also tell of clerical standing. In 986 *Ioruert*, Elri chose the two central words flanking the small cross to hold a validated split reading of EPISC, the widely-found abbreviation of *episcopus* "bishop". It is placed within ..SEPULCRIS IUDICII.. and looks like this;

$$\text{s / EP ulcr IS (+) iudi C / ii = EPISC}$$
$$\qquad\;\; 4 \qquad\qquad\quad 4$$

The span has thirteen letters, eight within it being unused, while EPISC has five; we find 5:8 → 13, from 1.2.3.*5.8.13*.21.34. Mentioned earlier was the commemorative stone from Caldey Island, shown in Fig. 5, from the time of Catgocaun king of Dyfed early in the 8th century. The text is riddled with acrostics shown by a series of grids. They identify the author as UNBO, but also tell us that he was ABBAS IESU NOMINE "abbot, in Jesu's name" of the monastery on Caldey.[60]

Inscriptions for kings, one might think, would for preference be written by their attendant bishops, and it has already been suggested that at Llangadwaladr – a royal foundation – the composer should have been of this grade. On comparable monuments in Spain and Portugal, overt (not encoded) references to bishops are found three times as EPISC, like Elri's self-allusion, and four times with another accepted shortening to EPS.[61] One might envisage Issiu favouring the latter because it avoids the 'C' of CATAMANUS. The LaN value of E P S, 5.14.17, is also 36, perhaps further favouring the last thirty-six letters as a repository.

Like Elri – though there can have been no direct link here – Issiu chose the central two words of his text and, in the span, separated letters with two equal intervals. We can read;

$$\text{sapi / E ntisimus o P inatisimu S / omnium regum = EPS}$$
$$\quad\; 4 \qquad\quad 9 \qquad\qquad 9 \qquad\qquad\qquad 11$$

with 21 letters in the span. The extreme-ratio validation comes as 15:21

$\rightarrow$ 36, which is times-3 from the convention *5.7.12.19.31.50*. And there is no difficulty in accepting this subsidiary announcement. Posterity was meant to realise that Issiu wrote with due authority.

The purpose of the messages in code

If the reconstructed circumstances leading up to the production of 970 *Catamanus* are thought likely, and many arguments support them, one might now ask; Why should its composer have gone to such lengths, encoding his name three times and adding his episcopal rank in only six words, when at the time his authorship of the commissioned inscription must have been common knowledge? Why bother?

Several responses come to mind, the most trivial being that he was prompted by vanity. These self-references are not however unique to a minority of early Insular inscriptions. An analogy is offered by those impressively large 17th–18th century sculptured memorials displayed in parish churches. These too have massaged past realities. Marble busts capture with nobility and serenity the likenesses of bibulous old Admirals and bloated landowners, and one often reads Latin encomia in prose or verse below the portrayals. Families who engaged fashionable artists to design and carve these monuments would expect those artists to publicise such patronage. Taking a long-term view the artists customarily inserted their names in tiny capitals on a plinth; G. GIBBONS, or RYSBRACK SCULPT. Fame is evanescent, word-of-mouth a puff of smoke. They were claiming their workmanship for posterity and so too, very likely, was Issiu.

When used for inscriptions or longer writings with a strong mathematical component, composition in Biblical style offers its own guarantees for the integrity of a text. It has been described as both error-detecting and error-correcting. If on a stone one vowel in a name has flaked off and might contextually be either E or O, LaN values 5 or 13, it is probable that devices exploiting LaN additions will confirm which letter it is (and can only be). The extraordinary qualities of Biblical style, when one studies it at length, enforce a singular conclusion. These practitioners like Issiu and Elri and others, post-Roman British and Irish clerics, knew that in a sense they were writing for secular eternity – and would have been aware that a restricted circle of readers knew the same. The means were there through which, at any future date, the model texts could be recovered, if necessary deciphered and made to yield images, and be wholly understood.

In this belief they were right, and the passing of a millennium or so is not material. Issiu, supposing that his tenure of office and own name would be forgotten a few generations on, incorporated what amounts to his signature. At the same time, while obliged to commemorate king Cadfan with extravagant praise, he made sure that a very different idea of Cadfan's real character and weaknesses was preserved – hidden, naturally, and at differing levels, but never irrecoverably so.

But more thoughts must follow from this; as generalities, speculative inferences, not deductions from hard evidence, though to some extent prompted by commonsense. The first is that Issiu must have had confidence that nobody in the 7th-century Gwynedd royal circle, no ill-disposed rival intellectual within reach of Aberffraw and Llangadwaladr, could penetrate his spoof epitaph and place him in immediate peril. After all, had it been pointed out that the rearrangement into the twelve-by-four grid now exhibited all those contiguous letters, the fend-off would be that this was a most curious and unforeseen thing, that Latin words unduly shared certain letters and that anyhow his five-line display was a picturesque tribute. The second notion, frequently suspected in any study of these special inscriptions, is that an expert knowledge of all the secrets, the devices, the associated codes, of Biblical style was not common. By the 7th century it had become confined to clerical circles, to people familiar with Latin as well as some Greek and Hebrew, and was being taught and transmitted only at selected monastic centres. Secular royalty and aristocrats who may have learned some Latin in childhood would not generally be instructed beyond a certain stage.

One argument that tends to favour these inferences is the Cadfan stone itself. Its state of preservation is unusually good probably because (as earlier proposed) it was never left outside, deteriorating in the weather. Yet, at this royal church, would it have been left *in situ*, on public view, intact, had any hint of its scandalous innuendos and concealed gibes been even suspected? Would it not then have been defaced or pulverised immediately? The deduction, this time unshakeable, is that nobody saw through it.

More words and letters

Cadwaladr grandson of Cadfan was a Christian king, founder of at least one church, perhaps involved with monastic vows and in later Welsh sources remembered as *bendigeit* "blessed", Latin *benedictus*.[62] It is probable that he remembered enough Latin to follow the sense of readings from the Vulgate, certainly enough to read and understand 970 *Catamanus*. Kings who attended church services were presumably interested in Old Testament passages showing much earlier kings in a favourable light. King Solomon, famously, had been granted *sapientia* "wisdom" by God. *Dedit quoque Deus sapientiam Salomoni,* "God furthermore gave wisdom to Solomon", it says in I Kings, chap.4, and then that Solomon *erat sapientior cunctis hominibus* "was wiser than all men put together". Issiu's SAPIENTISIMUS may have meant different things to him and to Cadwaladr but, on the face of it, *sapientisimus omnium regum* is an advance on what the Old Testament claims. There is a down-side. Bishop Issiu would assuredly have known (but did Cadwaladr remember?) that in I Kings, chap. 11 v.1, Solomon also *amavit mulieres alienigenas multas* "loved many foreign women". In that respect he may have outshone Cadfan's achievements.

The rest of our analysis, our unmasking of Issiu's concealed and sustained attack on Cadfan's reputation, moves away from the mathematical adjuncts of Biblical style to become mainly literary. Because the first exploration will involve a very close scrutiny, not of the slab as a whole but of individual letters cut on it, this is an appropriate moment to affirm that in many respects the lettering of 970 *Catamanus* is eccentric. It was meant to be so. If Issiu served on Anglesey for any length of time as the Gwynedd court bishop, and could produce Cadfan's memorial, it might be expected that among the surviving Anglesey inscriptions another memorial attributable to him could be recognised. The sole comparable piece is 971, Llangaffo = *ECMW* 35.[63] It is a tall pillar of local schist, now 55 ins, 140 cms, high and housed in Llangaffo parish church (see map, Fig. 3). In the 18th century it stood some 250 metres south-west of the church and by 1846 had become a roadside gatepost before being rescued.[64] The upper part is damaged. There are ten short horizontal lines and the best reading is [G]VI / RNIN / FILIVS / CVVRIS / CINI / ERE / XIT / HVNC / LAPI / DEM, "Guirnin, son of Cuuris Cini, put up this stone". Nash-Williams commented that it is "apparently a personal memorial rather than a tombstone."[65] It is more likely to have commemorated an event like the consecration of a new burial-ground or chapel, Guirnin being the donor of the land, and the wording anticipates commemorations of donors on much later Welsh crosses like 985 at Llanhamlach, Brecon, *ECMW* 61. This, 10th–11th century, has *Moridic surexit hunc lapidem.* There are Biblical echoes; Genesis chap. 31, v.45 *tulit itaque Iacob lapidem et erexit illum* "And thus Jacob brought a stone and set it up".

The lettering, shown in Fig. 7, is so close to that of Cadfan's stone that the same script-pattern is obvious, again possibly marked or painted on the rather irregular surface to be meticulously cut. Was the pillar – the occasion, the donor's status – important enough for bishop Issiu to have been asked to compose a suitable inscription? It used a mixture of capitals and half-uncials. There are instances of A, E, M, N and X all cut at the same line-height (and shown here in Fig. 7, with 970 *Catamanus* letters for comparison). The solitary 971 Llangaffo 'A', from its LAPIDEM, was constructed with the same three strokes as the small second 'A' in CATAMANUS.

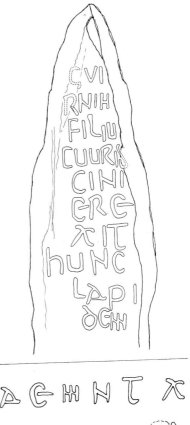

Fig. 7: Above, the 971 inscribed pillar now in Llangaffo church, drawn for the 1937 RCAHM Wales Anglesey volume (Crown Copyright); below, top line, selected letters from the Llangaffo inscription, compared with, bottom line, the same from 970 Catamanus. In the latter, the second 'A', marked A.2, exhibits the same kind of construction.

The other four much larger A's, in 970 *Catamanus*, are not matched, here or on any other inscription from Anglesey. Nor is the bizarre -EX of REX, in line 2 of the display, shown in Fig. 7 against the Llangaffo 'X' from EREXIT.

We will have to return to details of the Llangadwaladr lettering, but a conclusion begins to emerge. Aspects of the letters chosen by Issiu for Cadfan's memorial, as a final display, were deliberately enlarged and distorted and can only have been executed on the stone under his immediate supervision. A cutter, unable on his own to maintain regular line-height, would have been dismissed for incompetence. There is no objection to taking 971 Llangaffo as a 7th-century piece, broadly contemporary with 970 *Catamanus*, or to seeing it as designed by Issiu. Doubtless other stones existed. While it is agreed that only a fraction of the post-Roman Christian population in western Britain was ever commemorated on stone – that fraction being predominantly male and emphatically from the upper reaches of society – it must also be a sad fact that what survives is likely to represent, at best, no more than five or ten per cent of all such inscriptions.[66] And, today, distressingly few are in such good condition as Cadfan's slab.

A parting kick below the belt

Before leaving a recital of Issiu's ingenuities and progressing to a second, and more intellectual, enquiry it is worth recalling that there are other Biblical-style inscriptions which can be shown to generate images, and that not all confine themselves to a single image. In 986 *Ioruert*, of much the same date, a 36-letter square appears twice appropriately labelled, once as David's city of Jerusalem and then as a ground-plan of the Holy Sepulchre. Viola's epitaph for Carausius, the earlier 393 shown in Fig. 5, generates five or six little "pictures" including both plan and profile of Carausius in his *congeries lapidum*. The later (AD 806; encoded date) 350 *Idnert* starts with a 64-letter square showing two cross-shafts set in the ground, one acrostically labelled IESUS, and eventually a most elaborate devised and fully-labelled profile of Golgotha and the Crucifixion.

The devised profile image of Cadfan on his back involved having the 48 letters as twelve across, four down. But the number 48 is also sixteen-by-three – perhaps too shallow for most depictions? – and of course both eight-by-six and six-by-eight. Experiment will hint at the last arrangement, which can be shown with numbered rows:

1	C	A	T	A	M	A
2	N	U	S	R	E	X
3	S	A	P	I	E	N
4	T	I	S	I	M	U
5	S	O	P	I	N	A
6	T	I	S	I	M	U
7	S	O	M	N	I	U
8	M	R	E	G	U	M

Since we are still (just) in the realm of acrostics, LaN, anagrams and the guiding-sequence 4.9.13.22.35.57, a practised eye will see that the initial and last letters in line 1, C A = 4, the same in line 8, M M = 22, all the letters in line 1 add to 35, and that TISIMU in lines 4 and 6 adds up to 83, which is – as we saw – the LaN value of CATAMANUS. Are these not clear indications to proceed? Is this the moment to get out the clean slate and knife-point again? This time there are only two vertical pairs, EE, fifth column and UU, sixth column, but a fine vertical IIII pillar in col.four. Oddly, columns of I's figure in some extremely simple devised plans from sixth-century north Welsh inscriptions – *CIIC* 387, 392, 399 and 402 – where the image may represent an approximately square grave-plot and the linear III, or IIII, the elongated grave or burial within it. Here we face something completely different, but something related to the previous image of Cadfan. Once more, ovals and circles are to be drawn around significant letter-grouping, thus:

1	C	A	T	A	M	A
2	N	U	S	R	E	X
3	S	A	P	I	E	N
4	T	I	S	I	M	U
5	S	O	P	I	N	A
6	T	I	S	I	M	U
7	S	O	M	N	I	U
8	M	R	E	G	U	M

The result is another view of king Cadfan posthumously erect, this time seen from a different direction. It is an *end-on* depiction. We are standing somewhere by his feet. The column of four I's is the *membrum erectum*, once again impressively vertical. The bottom corners on either side have M (or, left, possibly M R), suggesting that they represent cross-sections of his *membra* "limbs, legs". Like their owner they are supine, *membra supina*, as S O P I N A in line 5 almost reminds us. Lines 4 and 6, each with T I S I M U, add up by LaN to 83, and now we find that col. 5, M E E M N M I U, comes to the same total. These all either traverse or support the phallic pillar and, because 83 is the now-familiar LaN value of the name CATAMANUS, they leave very little doubt as to the shameless possessor of the emphatic organ.

This is a second devised profile, of a most unexpected sort. It may not be as impressive as the twelve-by-four, sideways, picture, nor is it anything like so elaborately labelled; but does that render it any less convincing? Could that column of four I's have occurred purely by chance?

Yet even this exposure of Cadfan's proclivities when alive, coarse as it is, cartoon-like in its aggrandisement of his parts, may not complete the pictorial onslaughts. The side-view profile thrust upon us by the model's twelve-across, four-down, grid, and now the end-view added to it in similar fashion, constitute – as has been explained – *devised* images because they can only be shown through the simple device of rearranging the 48 letters. There are other, considerably less offensive, exploitations of Welsh inscriptions that yield devised images which one finds, after the most careful scrutiny, may be heralded by "ghosts", almost hints towards pictures, inherent in the displays and requiring no more than a prolonged stare to reveal their nature. A memorial set up by her father for a young girl, 421 *Rostece* from Montgomeryshire, yields a seven-by-seven letter square depicting a cross set in the ground, the letters of her name pendant from its horizontal arm, and apparently her memorial pillar to one side. The stone itself, unaltered as anyone sees it with its seven horizontal lines, also contains a potential linear cross which is conveyed by the horizontal tops of certain letters, the vertical elements in others, and an 'O' at their intersection. Contemporary with 970 *Catamanus* is the previously-cited memorial from Llanlleonfel, 986 *Ioruert*. One of its two devised images is a ground-plan, duly labelled, of the Holy Sepulchre; only after working this out does one realise that on the visible face of this large slab, in the actual display, the devised plan is foreshadowed by a display plan with exactly the same theme.

The potential existence of something similar here was borne in on the present writer, an archaeologist familiar with human skeletal anatomy who has had to excavate many Early Christian and medieval skeletons in fairly complete states, by a nagging resemblance between the inscription's enlarged uncial A's and the two foramina, the holes or apertures, at the base of the human pelvic bone. Fig. 8 shows why.

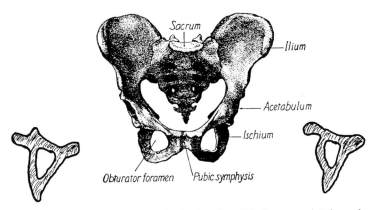

Fig. 8: Centre, from an anatomy textbook, drawing of the human pelvic bone showing the two holes or foramina at its base. Flanking, two selected A's from 970 Catamanus.

When reconstructing the activities that could have led to a placing of the slab in Cadwaladr's new little church, over the re-buried remains of his grandsire, it had to be posited that Cadfan's original grave – at Aberffraw? – was both identifiable and accessible. May we suppose that it was discreetly opened, the capstones lifted from a stone-lined cist for instance, some days or even weeks before the necessary *translatio*? Cadfan, interred 30 or 40 years earlier, would be represented by his skeleton, accompanied or unaccompanied by any grave-goods, the bones being still articulated; i.e., in their right relative order and positions. During removal they would almost certainly be disarticulated, jumbled up, but in viewing any human skeleton lying on its back most people are struck by the size of the skull, the apparent profusion of ribs and the prominent pelvis.

Appalling as this may seem as yet another gross impiety, it can be suggested that the composer's decision to frame his text in half-uncials instead of capitals was – apart from the bonus of uncial A's to serve as donkey's ears, and the copulating EX – to some degree influenced by the resemblance of these letters to skeletal components. The slab lies flat (as indicated in Fig. 6). We stand at one end, and look along it, along the lines of letters, the Cross at the far end. More than half-way down, the letters A.2 and A.5, if set a little diagonally, stand for the foramina of the pelvic bone. The whole inscription, so viewed, becomes perverted into a display image of the skeletal Cadfan; Fig. 9 illustrates this. An oval, outlining the Cross, is the skull. Top left, the stub of line 5, is the UM of REGUM. Is it at the same time h)UM(erus, *humerus* "a shoulder"? Then the two vestigial legbone assemblages have to be, line 1, right, M A N U S, and from line 3, left, T I S I M. Far, far more awful is the revelation of what lies between

Fig. 9: A display image inherent in the lettering; the inscription as seen by a viewer standing at its non-Cross or right-hand end. Outline of Cadfan's skull is marked by the Cross, and the two hatched A's are the foramina of his pelvic bone. Other features are explained in the text.

them. The bone bridge on a pelvis between the foramina is the pubic symphysis. For this image, there is (line 2) a P, root of the letters P I E N T I S I. In no possible way can these represent any bone. What they do conceal, and not very much, is a dispersed reading; **P** i **E N** t **I S** i, *penis*, in Latin meaning precisely that and, to some authors, a metonym or transferred sense for "lust" or obscene humour. And let us play the game to its dark end. PIENTISI is eight letters, five are used, three are not; 3:5 → 8 is extreme-ratio validation, 1.2.*3.5.8*.13...

There is no need to pursue this potential display image. Isolated, it would be too far-fetched to include in the search. Nor is it clear if, or how, it could have been accommodated with the other, devised, images. As a portrayal of Cadfan, however, it is anything *but* isolated.

Part Three

Donkeys on Parade

The tale of King Midas

The story of Midas king of the Phrygians comes to us in Book XI of Ovid's *Metamorphoses*.[67] Having befriended Silenus, elderly tippler and one-time tutor of the god Bacchus, Midas was told by the grateful Bacchus to choose himself a gift. Greedily and very stupidly, the king asked that everything he touched should be turned to gold. This baneful privilege was granted. Having spent a happy morn transmuting a twig, a stone, some earth, ears of wheat, an apple and parts of his palace, Midas broke off for lunch; but was horrified to find that he could consume nothing, even the bread and wine becoming gold as soon as he touched them. Entreated by the desperate monarch, Bacchus cancelled the gift. Midas, sickened by riches, retreated to the wild countryside. His next mistake was to interfere in a musical competition between Pan, whom he worshipped, and the lyre-playing Phoebus Apollo. The mountain-sage Tmolus judged Apollo an easy winner. Midas made a great fuss, declaring the verdict unjust. Apollo would not permit ears so foolish to retain their human shape, and turned the *aures* of Midas into the long grey hairy pointed ears of a lumbering ass. The shamed king had to hide his head in a purple turban but one man – the barber who trimmed Midas's hair – knew the secret. Eventually, unable to keep it to himself any longer, the barber went out and dug a hole in the ground, into which he whispered the secret before filling the trench in. But a thick carpet of reeds grew up on that spot, and betrayed the man. When fully grown they rustled in the wind; the reeds whispered the words buried below them.

Any bright child lucky enough to have had a full three-stage schooling,

Roman style, in post-Roman Britain and Ireland would have encountered the works of Ovid. The Latin of Publius Ovidius Naso, 43 BC to AD 17, pagan though he was, stood high as a Classical model for the next two millennia and the *Metamorphoses* contain many great tales. There were Insular imitations, certainly of the Midas episode, making allowance for the fact that the ass – a North African species first domesticated around the Mediterranean – was probably rare in Roman Britain and almost unknown in parts of Wales or in Ireland. One story involves the Welsh king March son of Meirchyawn, who had horse's ears – *march* means "horse" – and a similar version is known about an Irish king Labraid Loingsech.[68] Issiu must have encountered Midas in the *Metamorphoses*, and may indeed have known an early form of the March story in Gwynedd, where the barber entrusts his secret to the earth. Reeds grow up there, are cut and made into pan-pipes but at a royal feast they can play nothing except "March ap Meirchion has horses' ears".

The male donkey, *asinus* in Latin (so to Ovid, and thus to Issiu), has been saddled with two characteristics. One, most unfairly ascribed, is its stubborn stupidity – donkeys are much more intelligent than horses. The other is described by an authority on the domestication of animals in prehistory; "The sex life of the ass is spectacular and full of temperament, hence it is only natural that there should be frequent allusions to it" (i.e., in classical literature).[69] We all know that unworthy temptation to despise those we think we have outsmarted, as Issiu seems to have outwitted Cadwaladr. We cannot know, of course, if Issiu chose to think that Cadfan had been as dim as his grandson but, having dealt so picturesquely with the late king's physical endowment, the composer repeated and expanded his assault in this particular direction, and did so on Ovidian lines.

Asinine insinuations

The opening shot was a small salvo of anagrams. The two single-S superlatives were wheeled out. OPINATISIMUS is readily resolved into OPTIMUS ASINI "the best [bit] of an ass", some masculine noun like *ornatus* "embellishment" being implied. No prizes are offered for guessing *which* bit the composer had in mind. SAPIENTISIMUS likewise yields IPSE ASINUS T I M "Himself, the ass – T I M". The subject is identified because T I M, LaN values 18.9.11, adds to 38. In either Arabic or Roman numerals it is the converse of another number, thus: 38 = XXXVIII = *triginta octo*, while 83 = LXXXIII = *octoginta tres*. But '83', as we have now seen often, is the LaN value of CATAMANUS.

Because the inscription has only 48 letters it is not quite a letter-square (as 49, seven-by-seven), but worth setting out:

C	A	T	A	M	A	N
U	S	R	E	X	S	A
P	I	E	N	T	I	S
I	M	U	S	O	P	I
N	A	T	I	S	I	M
U	S	O	M	N	I	U
M	R	E	G	U	M	*

Encouraged by noticing that cols. 2 and 6 both start with ASI [nus?], we can look at the telestich, col. 7. NASIMU is the anagram of ASINUM – *asinum*, accus. of *asinus*. One cannot rule out a possibility that more tortuous rearrangements of the text would produce further "donkey" anagrams. These can suffice. Some pictorial vignettes await our scrutiny.

The illustration below reproduces the 970 *Catamanus* display, with its five uncial A's numbered for reference and three other features arrowed, marked (a) (b) and (c). Readers can now emulate post-Roman visitors who

Fig. 10: The inscription, emphasising certain letter-forms. The five A's are numbered for reference; encircled a, b, c, arrowed, indicate other features.

saw the display and were no doubt perplexed by many of the uneven letters. At this period Insular *capitalis* often showed reduced-size letter 'O' – arrowed (a) – but remembering that the O(pinatisimus) over the O(mnium) stood for *oculi* "the eyes" the small doughnuts can pass muster. Not so the word REX, line 2, arrowed (b). The medial bar of the E has moved over to become in effect a fifth limb of the conjoined X. One has to say that it looks for all the world as if this X has managed to acquire its own *membrum sexuale* and is busily penetrating the cringing part-E. To the left the letter R of REX, so much bigger than the opening R of REGUM, end of line 4, almost resembles a set of male genitalia, butting against the copulating EX. And what about the foot-terminal of the Cross – arrowed (c) – which differs from the other three terminals, Fig.2, in being so bulbous?

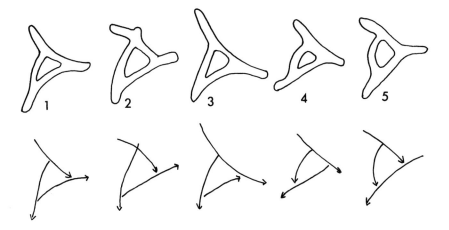

Fig. 11: The inscription's uncial A's, numbered as in Fig. 10, and here drawn out separately from enlarged photographs. Below, the apparent construction-lines as they may have been penned in the composer's model, showing how A.4 and A.5 are different from the rest.

The five uncial A's, a distinctive letter derived from a capital and quite different from the half-uncial, which is closer to our own "lower case" handwritten letter, have been numbered.[70] What appears in the display on the slab must be one remove from anything originally penned by the composer; however, in most respects these A's should be accurate

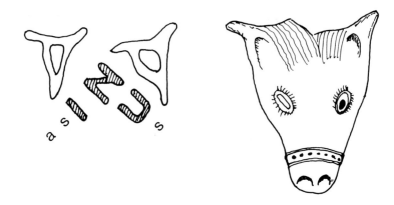

Fig. 12: A detail from the middle of lines 2, 3 and 4 in the inscription; letters A.4 and A.5 become the ears of an ass, (as)INU(s).

reproductions from his pattern, perhaps painted-on by him. Their constructions differ. Uncial A is made with three strokes to give an enclosed triangular shape but, as with characters in Chinese, it should be possible to detect the pattern and order. Fig. 11, with arrowed strokes, show how each was done.

Now it is seen that A.4 and A.5, in sApientisimus, opinAtismus, differ from the others, as they also do because A.5 sprawls across lines 4 and 5 of the display. In the supine-Cadfan image, A.4 and the opening A.1 stood for Cadfan's *aures* "ears". A.4 and A.5 are about to mean the same. For the solution, a small display-profile image, turn the inscription 45 degrees to the left. The A's become the ears of a donkey (Fig. 12 above). They are even partly labelled. The other letters below and between them, I N U, belong to [as]INU[s], "ass". The message of this, the latest little devised profile, is driven home with yet another textual device, a pair of validated split readings, so:

catam / **A** n **U** s **RE** x **S** / apientisimusopin / **A** ti **SI** musom **NI** / umregum
　　5　　　　8　　　　　　　16　　　　　　12　　　　　　7

– giving AURES ASINI, "ears of an ass". The spans have 20 letters, those unused coming to 28, with a total 48. This gives 20:28 → 48 which, divided by four, is extreme ratio as 5:7 → 12, from *5.7.12.*19.31.50.

Sharp-eyed readers will have spotted, naturally, that AURES ASINI can also be read thus:

catam / **A** n **U** s **RE** x **S A** pienti **SI** musopi **N** at **I** / simusomniumregum
  5   27   16

and one can even detect the donkey's other relevant organ, in:

catamanusrexsa / **P** i **EN** t **IS** imusopin **A** ti **SI** musom **NI** / umregum
     14   27   7

But while the composer probably noticed these, neither is validated. Their spans divide as 10, 17, 27, and their placings as 21, 27, 48. In neither case are these figures in extreme or mean (or other) ratio. If we are to play the game according to the rules, only the first AURES / ASINI reading stands. Note how the preceding and following unused letters, 5 and 7, offer 5:7 → 12, the extreme ratio that occurs times-4 in the whole placing; the two separated spans, one with AURES the other with ASINI, correspond to the two ears, and the 'A' of ASINI is A.5 (from opin**A**tisimus), the large "ear" that straddles two lines.

Whispering Reeds

The referral of dead king Cadfan to selected aspects of Ovid's King Midas is carried out with such perverse ingenuity that one can hardly doubt the composer's acquaintance with *Metamorphoses*, book XI. The theme of sexual excess had already been exploited; one assumes stupidity as the opposite of *sapientia* rather than, as Ovid implied, deafness to the finer things of life like Apollo's music, is the message here. What might also be read is that, in his knowledge of dark secrets about the departed Cadfan, Issiu was placing himself in the position of Midas's barber. The grave within the church at Llangadwaladr is the barber's hole-in-the-ground, duly filled back when the slab was laid over it. The forty-eight letters on the stone's surface reproduce or perpetuate the composer's own model, very likely penned in ink on a spare piece of vellum. A pen could be fashioned from a reed, *calamus*. Ovid's telltale plants were the species *harundo* – elsewhere, the sort used to make musical pan-pipes – but in Classical Latin *calamus* and *harundo* meant very much the same. Not at once, but in the fullness of time, all those strange letters would become as reeds themselves, whispering in the breezes of too-close inspection and interpretation, telling the buried secrets. And from what Ovid says, or does not say, we have to assume that Midas's barber, too, escaped consequent punishment.

Part Four

To Bobbio – And Back Again

Clues, inferences and deductions

There was a theatrical streak in Sherlock Holmes. Dr Watson could be a convenient one-man audience as well as a companion, and Holmes often played to him like a stage magician. "It is not really difficult to construct a series of inferences, each dependent upon its predecessor and each simple in itself," the Great Detective once remarked. "If, after doing so, one simply knocks out all the central inferences and presents one's audience with the starting-point and the conclusion, one may produce a startling, though possibly meretricious, effect." To Holmes the words "inference" and "deduction" meant the same – the process of logical reasoning from data or his own close observations, leading step by step to a conclusion.

In the present study all the central inferences have been left in and it is to be hoped that whatever conclusions have been reached are supportable. For the picture of Cadfan frozen supine on stone the clues to the image in its twelve-by-four grid were the transparent disguise of the five lines, the chiasmus, the paired and tripled letters, their correspondence to words for parts of the body in Latin and the allusion, *via* Gildas, to Maelgwn's reputation. For the revelation of the composer's name the clues were pointers to a series 4.9.13.22.35.57, presence of precession-and-interval readings, a separate emphasis on the number seven and to some extent the analogy of concealed auctorial names in comparable Insular texts. For the correlation with Ovid's Midas the clues were the irregularity of the letters, the oversized A's, various anagrams and acrostics and the not very deeply hidden references to *asinus* and *aures*. This, in sum, is how the relatively few but unquestionably impressive, top-grade, inscriptions composed in

Biblical style work. Between them they exhibit this range of devices, literary tricks, computus and cryptograms, and they make it clear too that their composers were familiar with Latin sources, secular and religious, over and beyond the Vulgate.

We have encountered enough to infer that Issiu, an *episcopus*, was naturally at home with his Bible[71], knew the *De Excidio* of Gildas and the *Metamorphoses* of Ovid. Those cannot possibly represent the extent of his Latin reading, though there is a limit to what can be deduced from any message of only six words. However, 970 *Catamanus* exudes convincing, and surprising, evidence for his knowledge of a fourth literary source and we must preface our continued enquiry by turning to a very different category of Latin writing.

Plays in living Latin

Enough has survived from Roman Britain – scenes and brief texts on mosaics, the odd piece of verse on personal memorials – to confirm that schooling in Latin was based on the expected repertoire of the major writers; Cicero, Vergil, Ovid, Horace and a few others. In the early 7th century Issiu and others, if they experienced formal schooling somewhere in the Insular world, would have been taught from the same models. Yet we can overlook that, in early Rome or Ravenna or Constantinople or the more enlightened Latin-speaking provinces of the Empire, most people did not – *could* not – speak in the manner of Cicero, whose magisterial and resounding command of the language and a huge vocabulary placed him on a linguistic peak. Similarly, in 18th-century London ordinary folk never conversed at the level of another great orator, the Anglo-Irishman Edmund Burke, 1729–97. In the following century Charles Dickens was capable of writing in top-register English at the same level as Burke's deliveries, but our debt to Dickens (at any rate, a socio-linguistic debt) is because he also gave us a record of bottom-register, Cockney and Home Counties, speech through his Sam Weller, Mrs Gamp and dozens of others.

In the Roman world the nearest equivalent to a Dickens was the dramatist Titus Maccius Plautus, born around BC 250, died about BC 184. Plautus was bilingual. He adapted and transformed Greek-language plays for the Roman stage, with hosts of vivid characters, plenty of action and a sparklingly original handling of colloquial Latin. These quick-fire dialogues and interjections are set in the mouths of courtesans, shop-assistants, misers, soldiers, nurses, dubious businessmen, pimps, layabouts and other denizens of city life. Many of his plays have a knockabout, "Carry On Up The Forum" quality. Plautus gives us what may be the closest we could ever hope to get to Latin as a living speech, a long way from the polished converse of Cicero and his friends.[72]

Pseudolus, a title made up from *pseudo-dolos* "The Make-Believe Slave", is one of the later comedies. The anti-hero Pseudolus is a domestic slave in name only, a Mr Fixit to Simo, who is a rich but mean Athenian. Simo has a not very bright son Calidorus, kept short of pocket-money by his stingy father and dominated at all times by Pseudolus, who acts as his grossly unsuitable mentor. Calidorus is in love with a singing-girl Phoenicium (described in the play as *meretrix* "a strumpet") who is however penned up in a popular downtown brothel run by Ballio, another heartless rogue, and frequented by the military. The storyline mostly concerns attempts by poor Calidorus to purchase his sweetheart's freedom, in which he is helped by every sort of trick and swindle that Pseudolus can think up. This précis of the play can emphasise how far removed we are, in literary tone, from the flowery elegance of Horace's Odes or the *Aeneid* of Vergil, and unimaginably further from Jerome's Vulgate or Epistles. By and large the comedies of Plautus – of which *Pseudolus* is typical – are about the last thing one would expect any bishop in post-Roman Wales to cherish in his private library.

From Athens to Anglesey

Now read these excerpts, which have been arranged under themes encountered in the disentanglement of 970 *Catamanus*. Translations may be colloquial, as they should be, but also literal.[73] A single correspondence might be shrugged off as an amusing coincidence; how many can we find?

Written letters copulating, like E and X in Fig. 8

Act I scene 1   (Calidorus has a wax-tablet note from Phoenicium, smuggled out of Ballio's whorehouse. He can't make out her writing, and has to show it to Pseudolus. Pseudolus can't make much of it either)

line 21   Pseud: *ut opinor quaerunt litterae has sibi liberos alia aliam scandit*
                   "Well, if you ask me, these letters are trying to make babies –
                   they're mounting each other!"

A supine human figure depicted by means of letters on a surface
                   (They continue to examine the tablet)
line 33   Pseud: *tuam amicam video Calidore*
          Cal: *ubi ea est opsecro*
          Pseud: *eccam in tabellis porrectam in cera cubat*
                   "I can see your girl-friend, Calidorus!"
                   "Oh? Where *is* she, I'd like to know?"
                   "Here she is, stretched out full-length on the tablet – she's
                   lying down on the wax!"

Conjunction of eyes and ears, as OO, AA in the supine-Cadfan image
                   (Calidorus has no idea what to do next, but clever Pseudolus has
                   hatched a plan)
line 122 Pseud: *de istac re in oculum utrumvis conquiescito*
          Cal: *oculum utrum anne in aurem*
                   "Leave this with me – you pop off and sleep soundly, on
                   whichever eye you like"
                   "On whichever *eye*? don't you mean *ear*?"

Men partly equated with donkeys, as in Fig.12, and for Midas
Act I scene 2   (Calidorus and Pseudolus have gone to call at the brothel. Just
                   as they get there, Ballio rushes out, chasing his slaves and
                   bellowing at them)
line 4   Ball: *neque ego homines magis asinos nunquam vidi*
                   "I've never seen men more like donkeys!"

A price for love
Act I scene 3   (Calidorus is back at the brothel trying to find out what has
                   happened to Phoenicium. He is horrified when Ballio finally
                   admits that he has just sold her to an army officer)
Line 110 Cal: *meam tu amicam vendidisti*
          Ball: *valde viginti minis*
          Cal: *viginti minis*
          Ball: *utrum vis vel quater quinis minis*
                   "You've *sold* my girl?"
                   "Sure – for twenty quid."
                   "For *twenty* quid?"
                   "Or four fivers, if you want to put it another way."

The first four of these edifying exchanges concern particular words or metaphors apparently common to the decoded inscription and the text of Plautus's play. The last extract is rather different. It contains three clues; 1, from *minis*, a unit of money whose name starts with M – a *mina*, silver coin worth 100 *denarii*; 2, a price of twenty; and 3, the figure twenty expressed as four times five.

What can this possibly have to do with Cadfan's six-word memorial? Of course four fives make twenty, as any obliging brothel-keeper would be glad to confirm. There are also marginal references to these three numbers in the inscription – the five-line display has a four-line model, CATAMANUS REX has five syllables and the name alone has four, the first and last letters of the name as C S, 3.17, make twenty, and so do the top and bottom letters of columns 1, 5 and 6 in the grid (C S again; M I,11.9; A U, 1.19). All of this is besides the point. We have to move from letters-as-numbers, LaN, to letters-as-*numerals*, LNu, the system where selected Roman letters, usually as capitals, were arithmetical markers – I, V, X, L, C, D, and M stood for 1, 5, 10, 50, 100, 500 and 1000. Within the text the letter for vowel /u/, in *capitalis* always V, occurs five times, probably fortuitously.

Let us now set out once more the 48 letters as twelve across, four down, putting the last letters in the lines as capitals for emphasis:

c	a	t	a	m	a	n	u	s	r	e	X
s	a	p	i	e	n	t	i	s	i	m	V
s	o	p	i	n	a	t	i	s	i	m	V
s	o	m	n	i	u	m	r	e	g	u	M

Those letters are meaningless as a telestich in any known language, but what if we take X and V in their LNu capacities? Do they make a little addition, like this?

X	*decem*	10
V	*quinque*	5
V	*quinque*	5
(= XX	*viginti*	20)

If so, the final letter M must tell what is being counted here:

M   *minae*

– and we are back with *viginti minae*, Act I scene 3, the price of a girl in Ballio's establishment.

The implication of these half-dozen close correspondences between Act I of *Pseudolus* and the developed text of 970 *Catamanus* may be beyond recovery (was Issiu suggesting, on top of everything else, that Cadfan had been no better than a stock figure of low comedy, or that he went in for buying loose women?) but the correspondences themselves cannot be ignored or dismissed. Nor is this all. Plautus was renowned for coining new Latin words and names. They enriched his dramas, and many of his neologisms were subsequently taken up and repeated in standard Classical Latin, even by Cicero. The comedies were immensely popular both on the stage and as light reading. St Jerome himself admitted that he read them constantly when young. In his *Menaechmi*, at a very much later time adapted by William Shakespeare as his own *Comedy of Errors*, Act I scene 2 line 35, Plautus produced "Catamitus" from the Greek *Ganymedes*.[74] Ganymede was the beautiful youth carried aloft by an eagle to serve as Jove's cup-bearer. Stark realism crept in. Cicero used the word to mean a catamite or pathic. The sense shifted to one of beautiful youths carried off by naughty old men instead of eagles. By 1593 if not earlier (so the *OED*) it had passed into English as "catamite", tersely defined as "a boy kept for unnatural purposes", or, in cruder modern-speak, a rent-boy.

A generation (or two) after his death in the 620s the complete gamut of Cadfan's sexual proclivities, as for those of his ancestor Maelgwn, must have been a topic of the most guarded conversation in royal circles. We have seen that the chosen spelling CATAMANUS, for CATUMANUS, provided a necessary A in the right position (for *Aures*) and possibly a required LaN total of 83 as well. With deference to Sir Ifor Williams, it had nothing to do with a 7th-century weakening of an unstressed second vowel. Did Issiu also work it in to make the name look more like "Catamitus"? Was this deliberate?[75] Is there a further clue, in that the missing letters – I T – are hovering in the second line?

C   A   T   A   M   A   N   U   S   R   E   X
S   A   P   (I)   E   N   (T) (I) S   I   M   U

And then, lastly, we have the superlative OPINATISIMUS, an obscure word that Issiu might have known from the Vulgate. Plautus was fond of *opinor*, verb, *opinio*, noun, but always with its older meaning, "I guess, it seems to me, my view is that..." *Opinio* is what someone believes or thinks, not some universally-accepted factual statement. On the slab, Cadwaladr and others might have been told that the *opinatisimus* genuinely meant "most renowned". That would be what they were intended to believe. Given the other diverse insults, the odds are that the composer intended the word ironically; "King C., supposedly (or so his family think) most 'renowned' of all kings."

Unless these assorted indications to the effect that Issiu, if he was the composer of the inscription, knew of the playwright Plautus and was familiar with (at the very least) Act I of *Pseudolus* can be shrugged off as a series of the most remarkable coincidences – including that very specific X V V M = twenty *minae* – we meet with a puzzle that would have taxed Sherlock Holmes himself. As there has never been a shred of evidence that these plays, so far removed in tone from patristic literature, were circulating in British and Irish intellectual Christian circles during the 7th century AD, one deduction becomes inevitable. Issiu had once read *Pseudolus*, but somewhere else. The problem is compounded because, with Plautus, one has a writer from the 2nd century BC whose works were largely lost or forgotten throughout much of the Middle Ages; and because any further inferences, or cautious guesses, about where Issiu may have been depend upon a better-informed discussion of his likely dates.

Columbanus, the works of Plautus, and Bobbio

The Irish monastic founder St Columbanus, or Columban (not to be confused with the slightly earlier St Columba of Iona), was born somewhere in Leinster around 543 and first educated at home. Later, as a youth, he decided to seek further schooling and to enter a monastery. He found his way north to Bangor on the shore of Belfast Lough, home to a strict establishment founded in 558 by St Comgall. Columbanus became a monk, was soon ordained and because of his talents found himself in due course the chief teacher in Comgall's monastic school. When he was nearly fifty he decided to seek a wider field. With a group of friends and disciples, he made his way to France. From then onwards, his active, often contentious

and always influential career on the Continent is well chronicled in a near-
contemporary biography by the monk Jonas, by details in Columbanus's
surviving writings and by other historical mentions. He was involved in
secular as well as ecclesiastical politics among the several kingdoms in much
of northern France and Switzerland, then ruled by a mosaic of descendants
of the Merovingian king Clovis, 466 to 511. In the Vosges mountains
Columbanus set up various new monasteries – Annegray, Luxueil,
Fontaines. In the latter part of his life he wished to make a final home in
Lombardy. With the usual band of followers, in autumn 612 he trekked
south across the Alps. By now in his late fifties, he was not given to sitting
still anywhere for very long. After a period in Milan where he was once again
mixed up in ecclesiastical wrangling, Columbanus grew tired of cities and
experienced a longing for solitude. In the Apennines there was a little ruined
church of St Peter, at a spot named after its nearby babbling brook (Bobbio;
hence the *monasterium Bobiense*). Here his last small monastic house came
into being and here soon afterwards on 23 November, 615, Columbanus was
laid to rest.[76] Bobbio, as his foundation, continued to grow and flourish.
This house was anything but intellectually isolated. Its community would
have held brethren from Austrasia (northern France), Burgundy and
Lombardy and also an Irish contingent, originating with the saint's own
companions and reinforceable from the homeland. Over the centuries the
Bobbio monastery, with its scriptorium, amassed quite a notable library.
People there read, copied and wrote books, mostly in Latin.

In older Roman literary circles, Plautus's output was much admired
either in performance or just as a good read. More than a hundred plays
were at various times attributed to him. Only twenty or so have come down
to us, though these are accepted as being genuinely his work. No thanks
at all for their preservation are due to the Christian Latin world, in which
these metric comedies could never have served as standard educational
models. Today our principal source for those surviving plays is a group of
10th–12th century Vatican manuscripts. For the West, Plautus was hardly
rediscovered until 1429.

But there is one much older fragment. In the standard working edition
of the Vulgate Bible the *index codicum*, the catalogue of manuscript sources
used to prepare the edition, starts with *A*, the Northumbrian Codex
Amiatinus now at Florence which dates from the 8th century and contains

both the Old and New Testaments. Among the lesser codices are two in the Biblioteca Ambrosiana at Milan; one, shelf-mark MS D.84 inf., has Chronicles, and the other, MS G.82 sup., Book of Kings. Both came from the library at Bobbio. The manuscript G.82 sup., whose index-mark or siglum is *m*, has been described as *s.VII ab Hiberno quodam* "7th century, apparently [penned] by an Irish hand".

Sometimes we find that these individual books of the Bible had been copied out, from an earlier example of the Vulgate, on sheets or folios previously used for another, not necessarily Biblical, purpose. These sheets could be a most useful source of costly vellum to be scraped clean(ish) and then to serve anew as high-grade copybooks for monastic labours. The Milan Ambrosiana G.82 sup. is one such; a palimpsest or overwriting, a recycled object. What it originally contained was a play by Plautus, written in what the great palaeographer E. A. Lowe thought was an Italian hand of the 5th century. At the same time Lowe identified the Old Testament upper palimpsest as characteristically Irish handwriting of the seventh century (Bobbio, remember, had been founded shortly before 615).[77]

The implications are clear. From somewhere roundabouts, perhaps the remains of a Late Roman country-house library outside Milan, the foundation at Bobbio had picked up at least one Plautine comedy and if so possibly a larger collection – not for their contents, but as a handy supply of writing materials; stored in a press or chest, and doled out when required to be used again in palimpsest fashion.

"I Perceive That You Have Been In …"

One of Sherlock Holmes's opening tricks was to glance surreptitiously at a visitor's footwear and, from the species of mud adhering, to say where he or she had just come from. (It would be interesting to have a hard, cold, *opinio* from a real geologist about this accomplishment.) Another was to spring geographical deductions upon the unwary. In *The Red-Headed League*, Holmes spells out to Watson several obvious deductions about their visitor Mr Jabez Wilson (– "has at some time done manual labour … takes snuff … is a Freemason"), claiming also that he must have been in China. This is because "the fish which you have tattooed immediately above your right wrist could only have been done in China. I have made a small study of tattoo marks. That trick of staining the fishes' scales of a delicate pink is quite peculiar to China." (Mr Jabez Wilson laughed heartily. "Well, I never!" said he. "I thought at first you had done something clever, but I see that there was nothing in it after all.")

According to Dr Watson, in an idle moment drawing up a list titled "Sherlock Holmes – his limits" (*A Study in Scarlet*), Holmes's knowledge of literature could be entered as " – Nil". This is unfair. Holmes knew Latin and could quote hexameters. Had he been available on Anglesey in the seventh century, hired by a Welsh ecclesiastical synod to investigate their miscreant colleague Issiu, accused of insulting the royal house and of having picked up pagan and indecent literature some place abroad, Holmes might have begun by glancing at Issiu's boots for any traces of alien mud, and at Issiu's forearms for tattooed designs peculiar to specific cities in Gaul. Instead, *we* have been glancing at Issiu's composition with its traces of Plautus's *Pseudolus*, and beginning to deduce that he must have read, memorised or even privately copied the first act of this comedy. That would have been earlier in the 7th century. Could he have done so at Bobbio?

A matter of chronology

It now becomes appropriate to state a belief – not a firm deduction, more like a balance-of-probability guess, and certainly rather more than a suspicion – that Issiu was not by birth and upbringing a Briton from Venedotia, but Irish. His name must be related to a group of Old Irish male names with shifting spellings; *Ísu*, *Íssu* (*Crist*), *Ísa*, *Íssa* (Vulgate *Iesu* "Jesus"), and *Essu* (for *Iosue* "Joshua"). Certainly the encoded "Issiu" takes precedence over the "Essiu", or Essa, in the *Tripartite Life of Patrick* (which looks like, but cannot be shown to be, the same name). A related guess is that Issiu hailed from the northern or north-eastern part of Ireland, rather than a part further away from Gwynedd and Anglesey, and that his ecclesiastical training had been at Bangor. It could be relevant that Belfast Lough and the Anglesey harbour of Holyhead, 110 miles or 190 kms apart, are connected by a near-direct sailing route and, in calm weather, an easy passage. There need be no suggestion that Issiu was a disciple of St Columbanus at Bangor, or ever met him. If he attended the monastery there, it would have been some while after Columbanus's departure to Europe. More hypotheses about Issiu's career

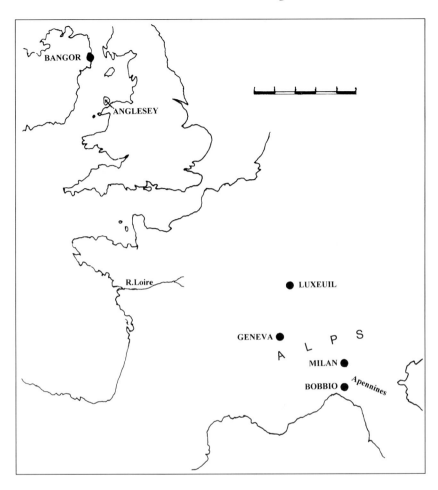

Fig. 13: Sketch-map, 7th-century western Europe; Bangor, Co. Down, to Bobbio, sailing from Ireland to the Loire estuary, crossing the Alps and returning via Geneva. Scale bar, 250 miles or 400 kilometres.

depend on dates, not regional geography. The map, Fig. 13, gives the setting of what is next to be discussed.

It would not be in the least unusual to find an Irishman, even as a bishop, in post-Roman Wales, or Britons and converted Englishmen in Irish monasteries, or Cornish people in south Wales, or Welsh and Irish figures in Cornwall. The seas were highways. Spoken Irish and the daughter-languages of British (Cumbric, Welsh and Cornish)[78] were no more mutually intelligible by now than Portuguese and French, but for the educated there was the common bond of Latin, language of the Church, the schools and the beginnings of historicity. At a minority level immigrants, emigrants and natives could compose, communicate and converse in Latin. Some friction was likely, then as now. The early 9th-century *Historia Brittonum*, a Welsh tract attributed to Nennius, repeated a tradition that Cuneda and his sons – ancestors of Cadfan, Maelgwn and other dynasties – had been moved from southern Scotland to north-west Wales in order to expel Irish settlers, and had gone on to perform the same services in the south-west, in Dyfed, Gower and Kidwelly.[79] The weight of evidence denies this. By 500, aristocratic descendants of Munster settlers were entrenched as the kings of Dyfed.[80] In Gwynedd, including Anglesey, the personal memorials include some with Irish names. The very name of the Lleyn or Llyn peninsula, the "pig's ear" south of Anglesey, comes from a word meaning "Leinstermen".

The focus of enquiry therefore shifts to the most likely dates for Issiu's life and career. Accepting, as this study has done, that he was the self-proclaimed author of 970 *Catamanus*, was the Gwynedd bishop at the time, may have been Irish and, if so, from the background that involved Bangor, Columbanus, Bobbio and an availability of the Plautine plays, what can we work out without transgressing the limits of reasonable inference?

For the three-generation Gwynedd line, Cadfan, Cadwallawn and Cadwaladr, father son and grandson, we noticed earlier those sources that allow the death of Cadfan before (all dates approximate to a year or so) 629; of Cadwallawn's during a battle in 634; and of Cadwaladr's from a pestilence in 664, rather than as late as 682. Foundation of a first church at Llangadwaladr, marked by a memorial to Cadfan that was not his contemporary upright tombstone but a secondary cover-slab for his translated remains, might be regarded as falling within a bracket of 650 to 663. A bishop advising, composing, and also consecrating the place would be aged at least 30 and more probably 50 to 60; in other words, a man born early in the century, say between 600 and 610. Training, induction to the priesthood, at Bangor (if not at some other Irish monastery) takes us to 620-plus. After that a pilgrimage to the Continent, alone or with youthful companions, would for any Bangor brethren be a journey facilitated by continuing links between the home monastery and Columbanus's foundations abroad. Visitors would carry letters, perhaps too some books as gifts. For the 7th century we have plenty of historical and archaeological evidence showing that voyages by trading-vessels direct to the mouth of the Loire were commonplace.[81] From Nantes, it is overland to the Vosges, and thence down into Switzerland, with a choice of passes over the Alps to northern Italy, the Lombard plain and the Apennines. Devout Irishmen would not miss the chance of a visit to Bobbio, founded a decade or so earlier, the place of Columbanus's passing. It becomes much less improbable that Issiu could have been there. If so, was he on departure presented with a few folios of (re-usable) vellum from the scriptorium's store – enough to contain an erasable copy of only the first act of *Pseudolus*? It might have been deemed expendable as an unworthy relic. It beggars belief, of course, that any young Latinist, however deeply committed to the Christian life, would have refrained from looking at the 5th-century text. After all, St Jerome – none other; translator of the Vulgate but owner of a beloved private library – had enjoyed many a good read of Plautus, and admitted so in his widely-circulated Letters. And one has to remark that Issiu's use of *Pseudolus* Act I, in considerable detail many years afterwards, must suggest that he did more than just peep.

One, earlier-mentioned, reason for seeing Cadfan as dead before 629 comes with the *Annales Cambriae* entry for that year, concerning an *obsessio* "siege" of *Catguollaun* = Cadwallawn, described as *rex*, which took place in the island of *Glannauc*. The reason to see this as a reference to some event on Anglesey, not necessarily at Aberffraw but at some defensive work memorably besieged by invaders, comes from a claim in Bede's *Historia* concerning the Northumbrian king Edwin, who reigned from 616 to 633. Edwin, on the war-path, conquered *Meuanias Brettonum insulas* "the Mevanian islands of the British". No date is given but, as it must have been *after* 616 and *before* 633, was it around 629? The islands, plural, have been taken as representing Anglesey and Man. Neither Bede nor *Annales Cambriae* inform us as to Cadwallawn's fate, if the *obsessio* succeeded. In one rather later Welsh source, Cadwallawn is reputed to have spent seven years of exile in Ireland; a hiatus in his reign that, if not in reality so long, could stand for a period of enforced refuge across the Irish Sea. The true sequence of events in the life of this warrior-king of Gwynedd, who certainly recaptured Anglesey and parts of Gwynedd from the Northumbrian invaders, is open to discussion and remains so.[82] It is the stay in Ireland – in the north of Ireland? – that provides an opportunity, either late in the 620s or early in the 630s, for Cadwallawn having met Issiu; and then, for whatever reason anybody chooses to put forward, having invited Issiu back to Anglesey either as a bishop or as a priest attendant upon the court who in due course became its bishop. Those familiar with Bede's *Historia* are bound to be reminded of Bede's royal hero Oswald, who reigned 634 to 642. Exiled when young by dynastic in-fightings, he spent some years with the Irish learning their language and absorbing their Christian ways and then, returning to the throne of an united Northumbria, placed his own bishop at Lindisfarne in the person of the saintly Aidan, an Irish prelate from Columba's monastery on Iona.

This reconstruction, and it cannot pretend to be stronger than historical possibility, would have Issiu on Anglesey in the early 630s; himself then not much older than the century. It means that he would never have met nor seen king Cadfan; would have known his son Cadwallawn; and would have known Cadwaladr from childhood. Three decades later a priest in this position would have been privy to just about everything concerning the House of Gwynedd.

A visit to old Geneva?

Yet one more little problem concerning the wording on Cadfan's stone remains to be tidied up. Ignoring, for the moment, the closing OPINATISIMUS OMNIUM REGUM as verbal embroidery, essentially the contents of the grave are identified in the tripartite formula, CATAMANUS REX SAPIENTISIMUS = (Name) – royal title – superlative adjective. No other Insular inscription matches this. The Yarrow Stone, p. 25 earlier, with its INSIGNISIMI PRINCIPES NUDI DUMNOGENI, apart from having the names as gen., not nom., could be claimed as the formula in reverse but there is no reason to see these two men as genuine royalty and the inscription is not a Biblical-style composition either. In Wales there are several other memorials to historically identifiable kings, without a superlative among them, and the word REX became usual only in much later pre-Norman commemorations.

On the way back, perhaps, having left Bobbio and crossed or circumvented the worst of the Alps, Issiu could have come to Geneva, anciently *Genava*; historic heart of the present city with its churches, impressive palace of the Burgundian kings and sixth-century cathedral. The most cursory guided tour, a priest pointing out the sights to visiting fellow-clerics, would have taken in a prominent and handsomely lettered building-stone, a *Bauinschrift* cut in monumental capitals.[83] Lost in the Middle Ages it was found by one of the city's gates in 1840, and commemorates an enlargement by royal gift of some area around the cathedral and palace. Cut in three horizontal lines it says (Fig. 14):

GVNDOBADVSREXCLEMENTISSIMVS / EMOLVMENTOPROPRIO / SPATIOMVLTIPLICATO

– *Gundobadus, rex clementissimus, emolumento proprio spatio multiplicato,* literally "Gundobad, most compassionate King; for his own spiritual reward, the spatial extent having been increased". This Burgundian king reigned from 480 to 516 and in the early seventh century the tablet would have been extra-visible and perhaps picked out, Late Roman fashion, in bright colours.

No words are run over here. The first line is complete, as is CATAMANUS REX in Issiu's model. The formula, Gundobadus / royal title / superlative adjective, all in the nom., offers a precise parallel. An Irish

Fig. 14: Geneva, Switzerland; commemorative inscription on stone tablet from some larger structure naming the Burgundian king Gundobad, 480 to 516. Musée d'Art et d'Histoire, Geneva, drawn here from photographs. The lettering is sixth-century capitalis with characteristic angle-bar A, drooping L, and open P and R. Three lines, the topmost GVNDOBADVS REX CLEMENTISSIMVS.

visitor to Geneva would have no reason to know about another slab at Merida, in Spain.[84] This one refers to the Visigothic king Chindaswinth, who reigned from 641 to 652; though somewhat damaged it starts with [CHI]NDASUINTUS REX PI......S, where the third word can only be the superlative *piissimus* "most pious". Both this stone and Gundobad's accord regal superlatives to rulers who may have been *reges*, but whose markedly Germanic, non-Roman, personal names are a reminder of the once-barbarian tribes whose ancestors had supplanted the Augusti and the consuls in the western provinces of the Empire. The Gundobad inscription looks very like a model – a sight committed to memory – encountered during a likely visit at the right time. It may seem far-fetched to see Issiu as an antiquarian snob, regarding any pretensions on the part of Cuneda's descendants as barbarian by comparison with the Irish royal houses, and as late-comers to the Christian faith; but did he deliberately draw on memories to borrow for the despicable Cadfan a three-word opening otherwise used for a grandiose Germanic barbarian? Where else might he have found it?

Catalogue of insults

Occasional tasteless hints that Holmes and Watson, so snugly ensconced in their Baker Street rooms and cosseted by Mrs Hudson, were in any way *gay* ignore the Master's recorded techniques for dealing with female clients. When Miss Violet Smith dropped by with a problem in 1895 (*The Solitary Cyclist*) Sherlock Holmes started to fondle her ungloved hand, admitting that "I nearly fell into the error of supposing that you were typewriting. Of course, it is obvious that it is music ... There is a spirituality about the face" – he gently turned it to the light – "which the typewriter does not generate." ("Yes, Mr Holmes, I teach music.") While hardly ranking as an exercise in deduction, the episode illustrates that subjective assessment is not necessarily always wrong. Looking at the end-product of Issiu's ungloved hand, one could commit the error of mechanically summing him up as an adept at Latin, widely read, the possessor of an excellent memory, a master of composition in Biblical style, and a man endowed with what some might call a sense of humour. The summary leaves too much, too many un-deduced conclusions, still to be explained. Gently turning all of the 970 *Catamanus* inscription and its prolonged analysis to the light (of inspiration?), does one detect an Irish quality present that the contents of similar British inscriptions do not generate? Is all this playing with words and letters – letters that add, have values, make numbers, move, couple, pair off, generate pictures and stand in for parent words – somehow anticipatory of James Joyce, George Bernard Shaw, and that genius Brian O'Nolan as "Myles na Gopaleen"?

None of this can explain, and to many it cannot excuse either, Issiu's treatment of Cadfan's memory. It stands unparalleled in the field of early Insular composition. From everything deduced and inferred and exposed and reconstructed, we are ready to put together a blow-by-blow catalogue, a *Collectio Calumniarum*, of the miscellaneous insults. Cadfan's *name*; whatever it had once meant in British, it was given a Plautine modification. "Battle-wise" or "Battle-Pony" becomes "Pretty Boy". *The first three words*; a swipe at a royal status that, however grandiosely phrased, was in reality as pretentious as that of any Germanic barbarian usurper. *The two superlatives* are satirical. "Wisest" is a mocking pointer to what Gildas had to say or, if to Solomon, then to that king as a lover of many foreign women, while "Most Renowned" carries an unwritten qualification "Yes, but who says so?". *The last two words*; in all carnal respects, possibly involvements with boys as well as women, Cadfan was no better than a punier version of king Maelgwn. *The four-line, supine, image*: a man so prey to lust that Death itself could not extinguish his desires, a man defiantly engaged in his very grave with some last-minute onanism. *The subsidiary, end-on, image*; looked at from any angle, Cadfan's most prominent feature was his permanent erection. *The asinine anagrams* and little vignettes; implications of stupidity and greed, like Midas, of the excessive physical endowment of a donkey, and possibly a reminder that someone else (Midas's barber; Issiu) was privy to the secrets. The grotesque irregular *letters* on the slab; more images of sexual activity, appropriate to donkeys. The assimilation to excerpts from Plautus's *Pseudolus*; an assertion that, viewed from the older superior world of real Classical learning, Cadfan's life merited nothing except derisive humour – for a sex-crazy provincial ass. And lastly the Biblical-style apparatus, the computus, that governs most of these revelations, so easy to operate if you happen to know the rules: an intellectual fire-screen, on the far or hotter side the pretentious simpletons who have to take their inscription at face-value, on this side their puppet-master.

How did it end?

The posthumous demolition of the late king Catumanus or Cadfan was so extraordinarily, so painstakingly, thorough that it raises once more a final deduction; bishop Issiu had for years and years been secretly smarting under some frightful grievance. When the chance came, he deployed his formidable skills to wreak revenge on what was only a memory. We can never know why. Even Sherlock Holmes could deduce nothing from the invisible.

Nor can one do more than guess how the story may have ended, though a few closing guesses are permissible. As explained earlier, it is in the nature of these compositions in Biblical style that everything, every device and detail and image, hidden and encoded could be resolved by using the relevant tricks in reverse. Plainly Issiu (or, if any reader still wants to deny his identification, whoever composed the inscription) knew of this possibility, and was prepared to risk it. The unblemished slab, the unexpunged wording, imply that it was a risk taken with impunity. One might infer that he felt safe in leaving any revelations to posterity.

There is a last possibility. Let us picture Llangadwaladr, its new small church, its prominent tomb, the royal gathering, at some date in the 660s. Bishop Issiu, if by today's measures a priest in late middle age, may have been an elderly man by those of his time. The completed slab, sharply lettered and faithfully reproducing its composer's model, had been placed over Cadfan's jumbled bones. Was this also an occasion for the bishop – his face impassive, but his eyes alert to king Cadwaladr's gratified inspection of Grandfather's epitaph – to tell his royal patron of a wish to make way for a younger man, and of a God-directed desire to pass the remaining years in monastic retreat; in his homeland, safely across the north Irish Sea?

It may strike readers, as more than once it has struck the writer of this book, a little sad that a composition of quite outstanding ingenuity is – at the same time, and in a strictly Christian light – a veritable monument of misapplied effort. Had poor Cadfan, about whom we know so very little from any source, no redeeming features whatsoever? What could he have done to deserve such obloquies? And later, pondering in his monastic cell back at Bangor or wherever, did Issiu wonder if a persistent enquirer, sooner or (as it has turned out) a great many years later, would manage to disentangle all his secrets? Did he *care*?

References

Place of publication unless otherwise stated is London. For broader treatment of certain topics a reference may contain a direction to Further Reading.

1. The Royal Commission on Ancient and Historical Monuments in Wales & Monmouthshire (= RCAHMWales), *An Inventory of the Ancient Monuments in Anglesey* (HMSO 1937, reprint 1960); Llangadwaladr entry, 85–8 with plan of church.
2. *Ibidem*, Appendix V, civ–cix, by C. A. Ralegh Radford.
3. So, e.g., J. O. Westwood, *Lapidarum Walliae* (Oxford 1876–79) at 190–1, with drawing pl. LXXXV fig. 4 – shown here in Fig. 1.
4. Accessible modern reprint, *Camden's Wales, being the Welsh chapters taken from Edmund Gibson's edn. of William Camden's Britannia, 1722* (Rampart Press, Carmarthen 1985), at 82. The slab was described as being "over the Church-porch", i.e. the south entrance.
5. RCAHMWales *Anglesey*, cviii no. 2; poor photograph, pl. 19.
6. See in next note; drawing, 56, fig. 21; poor photograph, pl. VII.
7. *CIIC* = R. A. S. Macalister, *Corpus Inscriptionum Insularum Celticarum*, 2 vols (Stationery Office, Dublin 1945,i, 1949, ii). *ECMW* = V. E. Nash-Williams, *The Early Christian Monuments of Wales* (Nat. Mus. Wales, Cardiff 1950). All references to inscriptions in this book use *CIIC* numbers and where possible the key name in italics.
8. *CIIC* 476, Rialton, Cornwall; BONEMIMORI = Latin *bonae memoriae*, equivalent to "In Loving Memory".
9. The phenomenon of Inscriptional Old Celtic spellings, or IOC, is examined in Charles Thomas, *Christian Celts. Messages and Images* (Tempus, Stroud 1998) (= *Christian Celts*), at 65–70.
10. Discussed by Sir Ifor Williams in RCAHMWales *Anglesey*, cxv, with conclusion that "So Cata- must be regarded as a late and poor tradition, which arose when the unaccented vowels in a word were becoming or had become slurred and obscure".

11. Sir John Edward Lloyd, *A History of Wales from the earliest times to the Edwardian Conquest*, 2nd edn, 2 vols (Longmans, 1921) at 181, n.86 on "Brythonic 'Catamanus' for an earlier 'Catumanus'".

12. Best general account of the Gaulish inscriptions, Jeremy K. Knight, *The End of Antiquity. Archaeology, Society and Religion AD 325–700* (Tempus, Stroud 1999), chap. 5.

13. So, influentially, Radford in RCAHMWales *Anglesey* at cv–cvi; "The lettering is the latest in the series in Anglesey. Date c.625."

14. Kenneth Jackson, *Language and History in Early Britain* (Edinburgh Univ. Press, Edinburgh 1953), 160–2, against Radford, "the Catamanus stone cannot be used thus categorically as an endpiece to the history of *inscriptiones Christianae*"; 512, "CATAMANUS (for CATAMANNUS)"; 620 n.4, "the undue (epigraphic) pressure exercised ultimately by the CATAMANUS stone", and 645, the name itself referred to British **Catumandus*.

15. *ECMW*, 57 n.3, some examples of Byzantine superlatives.

16. Frances Lynch, *A Guide to Ancient and Historic Wales. Gwynedd* (HMSO, for CADW, 1995), 117–8, better photograph than usual.

17. Daniel Stashower, *Teller of Tales. The Life of Arthur Conan Doyle* (Allen Lane, Harmondsworth 1999). A photograph of Joseph Bell appears, opp. 177, in Owen Dudley Edwards, *The Quest for Sherlock Holmes* (Mainstream, Edinburgh 1983).

18. In the short story *The Adventure of the Dancing Men*.

19. A crude "Arthurian" forgery was, no doubt unwittingly, included in Chris Barber, *More Mysterious Wales* (Paladin, 1987, at 144). Obvious and illiterate, it part-imitates *CIIC* 409 *Pumpeius*.

20. P. C. Bartrum, *Early Welsh Genealogical Tracts* (Univ. Wales Press, Cardiff 1966), Introduction, with Harl 3859 on p. 9, no. 1, and JC 20 on p. 47, no. 22.

21. Most recent treatment, R. Geraint Gruffydd, "From Gododdin to Gwynedd; reflections on the story of Cunedda", *Studia Celtica*, vol. 24/25 (1989–90), 1–14.

22. Its provenance is not known; discussion, Bartrum, *op.cit.*,41–2.

23. Comments on Maelgwn's dating, Michael Lapidge & David Dumville, eds., *Gildas: New Approaches* (Boydell, Woodbridge 1984), 51–9. For *De Excidio* see, text and translation, Michael Winterbottom, *Gildas. The Ruin of Britain and other works* (Phillimore, Chichester 1978). The date of AD 540 is by no means agreed but see David R. Howlett, *Cambro-Latin Compositions* (Four Courts, Dublin 1998), 42–3, and elsewhere in Howlett's works.

24. The translations of Gildas are Michael Winterbottom's.

25. The fullest treatment of the early Gwynedd kings is by Rachel Bromwich in

her *Trioedd Ynys Prydein. The Welsh Triads* (Univ. Wales Press, Cardiff 1961), in the long fully-referenced section *Notes to Personal Names*, 263–524 – Catuan, 290; Catwallawn m.catuan, 293–6; Catwalad(y)r, 292–3, and also Cunedda, 313.

26. John Morris, *Nennius. British History and The Welsh Annals* (Phillimore, Chichester 1980) at 38–9, paras. 61 and 64. The "Welsh Annals" are the *Annales Cambriae* mentioned here.

27. Between these alternative death-dates of 664 and 682 it becomes a matter of cautious judgement, the earlier being preferred. Confusions about dates for these frequent plagues abounded; see note 346 in Richard Sharpe, *Adomnán of Iona, Life of St Columba* (Penguin Classics, 1995), at 348–9.

28. Amply shown in *Geiriadur Prifysgol Cymru, A Dictionary of the Welsh Language* (Univ. Wales Press, Cardiff, 1950 – in progress), at 2094 onwards, *llan* and all its compounds.

29. As pointed out by Rachel Bromwich, *Trioedd Ynys Prydein*, 292; Sir John Lloyd's suggestion, *History of Wales*, i.230, that he died as a monk in his own religious foundation overlooks lack of any evidence that Llangadwaladr was a full monastery.

30. The historical archaeology of Aberffraw and its immediate area as the Gwynedd royal seat is still only known in part; its tenurial history is given in Glanville Jones's "Multiple Estates and Early Settlement", pp. 15–40 in: P. H. Sawyer, ed., *Medieval Settlement. Continuity and Change* (Edward Arnold, Leeds 1976), and see now Neil Johnstone's survey "*Llys* and *Maerdref*; The Royal Courts of the Princes of Gwynedd", *Studia Celtica*, vol. 34 (2000), 167–210, with Aberffraw at 172.

31. *CIIC* 325 = *ECMW* 33, as "Llantrisant", with Fig. 36; RCAHM Wales *Anglesey* cix-cxiii, reading by Radford, discussion by Sir Ifor Williams.

32. In his *Cambro-Latin Compositions* (n.23 earlier), 26–7, finally dismissing the idea that Bivatisus was somehow from Gaul.

33. Useful guides to this overlooked topic are Giancarlo Susini, *The Roman Stonecutter* (in Italian, 1967; translated, Blackwell, Oxford 1973); David Kindersley & Lida Lopes Cardozo, *Letters Slate Cut. Workshop philosophy and practice*, 2nd edn (Cardozo Kindersley Editions, Cambridge 1990); and Harold Crossley, *Lettering in Stone* (The Self Publishing Assoc. Ltd, Upton-upon-Severn 1991).

34. F. Lynch, *Gwynedd* (n.16 earlier), at 118.

35. A rare instance, probably a flat or recumbent grave-cover at the time of burial and dating to around 700, comes from Madron, mother church of Penzance in west Cornwall. Almost 2 metres long, a heavy narrow slab in fine whiteish granite, one end has a peculiar expanded-arm cross with flat base, and below

it a 3-line inscription (VIR QONFAL FILIU [S] VENNORCIT), its axis "vertical" and at right-angles to that of the cross. The cross, lettering and linear ornament occupy the entire face; this never stood upright part-concealed in the ground. See Charles Thomas, *And Shall These Mute Stones Speak? Post-Roman Inscriptions in Western Britain* (Univ. Wales Press, Cardiff 1994), 291 and fig. 17.13.

36. Instances listed in Charles Thomas, *Bede, Archaeology, and the Cult of Relics* = *Jarrow Lecture 1973* (St Paul's, Jarrow 1974).

37. Howlett, *Cambro-Latin Compositions*, 19–20, pointing out that CVLTOR ...AEQVI is reminiscent of *aequi cultor* in Ovid, *Metamorphoses*, bk. V, 100.

38. Walburg Boppert, *Die frühchristlichen inschriften des Mittelrheingebietes* (Von Zabern, Mainz 1971), 31–3 illus.

39. D. José Vives, *Inscripciones Cristianas de la España Romana y Visigoda* (C.S.I.C., Barcelona 1942), with very full indexes.

40. More accurate than the *CIIC* (no. 515) drawing is the figure and reading in Royal Commission on the Ancient Monuments of Scotland, *An Inventory of ... Selkirkshire* (HMSO, Edinburgh 1957), no. 174 at 110–13.

41. See Sir Ifor Williams's essay "Wales and the North", chap.vi in: Rachel Bromwich, ed., *The Beginnings of Welsh Poetry. Studies by Sir Ifor Williams* (Univ. Wales Press, Cardiff 1980).

42. As do other aspects of these early Scottish inscriptions; Charles Thomas, "The Early Christian Inscriptions of Southern Scotland", *Glasgow Archaeol. Journal*, vol. 17 (1991–92), 1–10.

43. This is *CIIC* 986 *Ioruert* = *ECMW* 62; all references to it here are taken from the long illustrated analysis, Charles Thomas, *Silent in the Shroud: a seventh-century inscription from Wales* (Pinkfoot Press, Balgavies, Angus 1999).

44. Howlett, *Cambro-Latin Compositions*, 22–3, sets this out.

45. On relatively few Insular inscribed memorials, curtailment of a line or a clumsy splitting of words could be explained because a stone's surface shows flaws and irregularities where a line might be expected to continue, enforcing its deflection. Here, while the surface of the slab (the local stone, apparently) is not perfect, no such physical reason can be supposed. From photographic details alone, lines 3 and 4 could both have been extended and a smooth patch after REG in line 4 has room, and more, for the line 5 UM.

46. Introductory sections to all the works by David Howlett listed under *Further Reading* define and explain Biblical style. There is also a glossary with all the unfamiliar words, including some that have had to be newly coined, in Charles Thomas, *Christian Celts* (n.9 above), at the back, 209–15.

47. *Christian Celts*, chap.2, "The Roman Background", examples from York and Lullingstone.

48. The oldest Insular manifestation of this tradition can be found on the late 5th-century 479 *Cunaide* eleven-line memorial from Hayle, west Cornwall; analysed in Charles Thomas, "Christian Latin Inscriptions from Cornwall in Biblical Style", *Journal Royal Institution of Cornwall*, vol. 2 pt. 4 (1997), 42–65. It is detectable in several later Welsh inscriptions.

49. Michael Winterbottom's translation (n.23 above).

50. Ovid, *Metamorphoses* Book VI, 242 – an appropriate source! The naming of body parts revealed here, at most some 20 words, is necessarily much shorter than the only comparable Insular list; the catalogue in the seventh-century Hisperic *Lorica* by Laidcenn of Clonfert-Mulloe, Co. Laois. Its fantastic vocabulary uses only a few of the Llangadwaladr words – *caput, membra, iugula, torax, umbilicus* can be noted. The best edition is David Howlett's; his "Five Experiments in Textual Reconstruction and Analysis", *Peritia*, vol. 9 (1995), 1–50 at 6–18, with his later suggestion in *Peritia*, vol. 10 (1996), 68–9, that Laidcenn wrote this in 659. A mid-7th century date has long been assumed – Laidcenn died in or around 661, *Annals of Ulster*. The authorship and date of 970 *Catamanus* argued in the present study might just allow the inscription's composer to have seen the *Lorica* with its longer, if functionally very different, corporeal catalogue.

51. The concept of these generated mental images is quite new, first shown in detail by Charles Thomas, "The Llanddewi-brefi 'Idnert' Stone", *Peritia, Journal of the Medieval Academy of Ireland*, vol. 10 (1996), 136–83, with fuller definition and classification in *Christian Celts*, chap. 6. It was however known to Lewis Carroll and his illustrator Sir John Tenniel.

52. Shown in *Christian Celts*, 142–9, with figs. 56 to 62.

53. M(ontague) R(hodes) James, originally published in *Ghost Stories of an Antiquary* (Edward Arnold & Co., 1904). Steinfeld is real, a Premonstratensian abbey, and James had been studying glass in a chapel at Ashridge Park, Herts., which he thought came from there (a note kindly supplied by Paul Ashbee FSA).

54. For enthusiasts, a selection of works about early mathematics is included under *Further Reading*.

55. Other "backwards" readings are hidden in the Llanddewi-brefi, *CIIC* 350, *Idnert* memorial (see n.51); a *retrorsum* anagram leads to IDNERT, a *rursus* anagram to PISCIL, probably name of the person who slew Idnert (Iudnerth).

56. Very similar is the outcome of triangularisations on the 986 *Ioruert* stone (n.43 above) giving 96 = IORUERT and 88 = RUALLAUN. The study also includes, p. 40, an example from Jerome's Vulgate.

57. J. Gwenogvryn Evans & John Rhys, *The Text of the Book of Llan Dav* (Oxford 1893, reprinted Nat. Lib. Wales, Aberystwyth 1979), at 279.

58. Richard Morgan & R. F. Peter Powell, *A Study of Breconshire Place-Names* (Gwasg Carreg Gwalch, Llanrwst 1999), 123–4.

59. Pádraig Ó Riain, *Corpus Genealogiarum Sanctorum Hiberniae* (D.I.A.S, Dublin 1985), 118, entry 671.12, Book of Leinster. Cf. Kathleen Mulchrone, *Bethu Phátraic. The Tripartite Life of Patrick, I, Text and Sources* (R.I.A., Dublin 1939), 155, with *Essa is Bite is Tasach*. The evidence is far from conclusive and Old Irish "Essiu" as name, 12th cent., is only found here, but "Issiu" is equally rare in Old Welsh.

60. This inscription, *CIIC* 427 *Catuoconi*, is analysed in *Christian Celts*, 169–74; as well as the acrostic readings, triangularisation produces 144 and the same times-2, 288, while "Unbo" is found using 5.7.12.19.31 in a backwards precession-and-interval reading directed by validated anagrams of *rursus* and *retrorsum*.

61. See in the index to Vives, *Inscripciones* (n.39 above).

62. As in the Jesus College 20 pedigree earlier, p. 13, with its "Kadwaladyr vendigeit".

63. RCAHM Wales *Anglesey*, cvi, best drawing; Sir Ifor Williams on the personal names, cxiv. The function of this stone, which is not an ordinary memorial, is overlooked; it is dated early 7th century (Radford), from its resemblance to 970 *Catamanus*.

64. The present writer is most grateful to Dr Nancy Edwards, Bangor, for supplying a correct history of its movements and locations.

65. *ECMW*, at p. 65. It might be safer to describe it as a personal record commemorating some activity or gift.

66. This difficult topic is examined in *Christian Celts,* 61–2, and see also Nancy Edwards, "Early Medieval Inscribed Stones and Stone Sculpture in Wales: Context and Function", *Medieval Archaeology*, vol. 45 (2001), 15–40. Noteworthy is the very slow rate of discovery now of any new inscriptions in western Britain.

67. Mary M. Innes, *The Metamorphoses of Ovid* (Penguin Classics, 1955 and reprints), scholarly and very readable translation; 248–51.

68. References to both, Rachel Bromwich, *Trioedd Ynys Prydein*, 446–7; as a widespread folk-tale motif, certainly going back to Ovid's time, there are echoes of this in Cornwall and Brittany. Sir John Rhŷs, in his *Celtic Folklore. Welsh & Manx* (Oxford 1901), 439, 572, suggested a specific link between king March and *Mona*, Anglesey.

69. F. E. Zeuner, *A History of Domesticated Animals* (Hutchinson, 1963), at 381 (with "the beds of Roman married couples were often adorned with asses' heads").

70. Convenient illustrated guide to the various scripts; Bernhard Bischoff, *Latin*

Palaeography. Antiquity and the Middle Ages, transl. Dáibhí Ó Cróinín & David Ganz (C.U.P., Cambridge 1990), part B, "The History of Latin Script".

71. For instance, the rare word *opinatissimus* occurs in the Vulgate (Book of Judith, chap. 2 v.13; omitted from Authorized Version) describing a sacked city, *civitatem opinatissimam Meluthi.* Interestingly this was also used by the West Saxon Aldhelm, bishop of Sherborne (c.640 to 709), in his prose treatise *De Virginitate,* of the Old Testament David; cap. 53, *David opinatissimus regum*; and rather later by the Welshman Asser in his Life of King Alfred, written in 893. Cap. 76 of this Life refers to king Solomon; *in hoc pium et opinatissimum atque opulentissimum* (= "richest") *Salomonem Hebraeorum regem.* I am grateful to David Howlett, Oxford, for pointing these out. Issiu's choice of the word placed him in most distinguished company.

72. See, still, a fact-packed summary by the noted Plautine scholar E.A. Sonnenschein in *Encyclopaedia Britannica,* 11th (and best) edn, New York 1911, vol. 21, 828–30. A good appreciation of Plautus as playwright is the *Introduction* to Paul Roche, transl. *3 Plays by Plautus* (Mentor Classics 1968; reprinted 1984, by Bolchazy-Carducci, Chicago).

73. The present writer's translation; see the whole play in E. F. Watling, transl., *Plautus. The Pot of Gold and Other Plays* (Penguin Classics, 1965), 213 to end.

74. Menaechmus, wearing a dress pinched from his wife, strikes a pose and asks "Tell me, haven't you ever seen a picture on a wall, where the eagle carries off Ganymede" (*ubi aquila Catamitum raperet*) "or Venus gets off with Adonis?", and the context is meant to convey a rib-tickling *double entendre.*

75. With this, we have to look back at details of the twelve-by-four letters supine image, the possibility that the diagonal NNNN and the erect member SSS are actively involved with, top line, not MANUS "hand" but ANUS (!), the related possibility that Cadfan is being accused of a catamiting perversion (buggery), and lastly the precise words (*De Excidio*, 33) used by Gildas when attacking Maelgwn – *in tam vetusto scelerum atramento veluti madidus vino de Sodomitana vite expresso stolide volutaris.* Michael Winterbottom's translation was "Why wallow like a fool in the ancient ink of your crimes, like a man drunk on wine pressed from the vine of the Sodomites?" But Gildas's oblique Latin is capable of a very much nastier interpretation.

76. This is a précis of much the best summary, the "Chapter I. Biographical" in G. S. M. Walker, *Sancti Columbani Opera* (= *Scriptores Latini Hiberniae* vol. II) (D.I.A.S., Dublin 1957).

77. Lowe, in *Codices Latini Antiquiores,* vols. 1–11 & supplement (Oxford 1934–1971), vol. 3, p. 23, no. 344b (with comment "written doubtless at Bobbio").

The original MS, 345, contained *inter alia*, a scrap of Plautus' *Poenulus*. Lowe affirmed the seventh century in his *Palaeographical Papers 1907–1965*, 2 vols (Oxford 1972). Bischoff (in n.70 above; his p. 83, n.5) wrote that "In my view the question of the date of the upper script of the Plautus palimpsest ... has not been satisfactorily resolved" (but did not say why he thought so). If linked to Bobbio, the Biblical over-writing must be later than the date, shortly before 615, of Bobbio's foundation.

78. Cumbric, which seems to have died out in the Norman period, was the speech of north-west England and southern Scotland.

79. John Morris, *Nennius* (n.26 above), pp. 20–21 and 37 (sections 14 and 62). The usual calculation places "Cuneda's Move" around 400, allowing it to be Roman-inspired.

80. Charles Thomas, *And Shall These Mute Stones Speak?* (n.35 above), chaps. 4 to 7, sets out the abundant evidence for this.

81. Summarised in Charles Thomas, "*Gallici nautae de Galliarum provinciis* – a sixth/seventh century trade with Gaul reconsidered", *Medieval Archaeology*, vol. 34 (1990), 1–26. The Loire mouth is only one of several likely landfalls.

82. The siege, its place and date, the sojourn in Ireland and the likely sequence of events are discussed by Rachel Bromwich, *Trioedd Ynys Prydein*, 294–5. The unidentified island *Glannauc* may be Priestholm, but Anglesey itself is militarily likelier.

83. Photograph, p. 5 Abb. 2, in Walter Drack, ed., *Ur- und Frühgeschichtliche Archäologie der Schweiz*; Band VI, *Das Frühmittelalter* (Schweizer Gesellschaft für Ur- u.Frühgeschichte, Basel 1979).

84. Vives, *Inscripciones* (n.39 above), his no. 366 at p. 128.

Further Reading

Since Dr V. E. Nash-Williams (a Monmouthshire man, born 1897, died 1955) has been mentioned several times as an authority notably taken in by Issiu's prank, it is only fair to affirm that his *The Early Christian Monuments of Wales* stands as a massive accomplishment, the product of some twenty years' labour only now in the long process of being replaced and updated by a fresh all-Wales survey. He was deeply religious, a High Anglican and active churchman, and has been spared the present work's revelations. An overdue study and tribute is Dr Mark Redknap's "On Broken Letters Scarce Remembred: Nash-Williams and the Early Christian Monuments of Wales", pp. 391–427 illus., in: Joyce Hill & Mary Swan, eds., *The Community, the Family and the Saint. Patterns of Power in Early Medieval Europe* (Brepols; Turnhout, Belgium 1998), an essay that merits careful reading.

The presence of Biblical-style composition in post-Roman and early medieval Insular writings, at first in Latin but then in several other languages, has only recently been recognised and described. Because it is unfamiliar and not always easy to understand, this compositional mode and the surprising skills of its earlier practitioners have not yet found their way into popular accounts of "the Dark Ages" or of so-called "Celtic Spirituality". Less excusably, Biblical style has been side-stepped and occasionally ridiculed by academics who seem to find straight rejection preferable to the hard grind of mastering its principles. For anybody wishing to persevere, straightforward accounts with definitions of the literary and arithmetical adjuncts prefacing a wealth of illustrative texts can be found in books by Dr David R. Howlett, all published by Four Courts Press, Dublin. Among them can be recommended his *The Book of Letters of Saint Patrick the Bishop*, 1994; *The Celtic Latin Tradition of Biblical Style*, 1995; and *British Books in Biblical Style*, 1997. Specifically Welsh in focus is his *Cambro-Latin Compositions. Their Competence and Craftsmanship*, 1998, chap. II of which analyses the literary figures (chiasmus, parallelism, metrical content, etc.) of a number of inscriptions including some mentioned in the present study.

Extension of Biblical-style composition to a minority of Insular inscriptions, much shorter than the manuscript texts examined by David Howlett, was first discovered in 1995, and then reported in a series of papers by the present author. Some are cited here in the notes or *References* above; n.43, n.48 and n.51. To these can be added, giving the *CIIC* numbers, "The Conversions of Scotland", *Records of the Scottish Church History Society*, vol. xxvii (1997), 1–41, expounding the image-generating 520 *Latinus*, Whithorn, and the associated 516 *Viventius*, 517 and 518, all three from Kirkmadrine; and, for a Cornish example dated AD 1007, *CIIC* 1051, *Penzance Market Cross. A Cornish Wonder re-wondered* (Penlee House Gallery & Museum, Penzance 1999). Much wider in scope, with a full treatment of "inscriptional" Biblical style and a first classification of the generated mental images, was: Charles Thomas, *Christian Celts. Messages and Images* (Tempus, Stroud 1998) – designed and written as an introductory handbook, and also showing pre-400 examples from Roman Britain.

A great many people are fascinated by numbers, their properties, their peculiarities and even their histories. The Venerable Bede was, for one; so too, presumably, bishop Issiu. Georges Ifrah's book *The Universal History of Numbers* (Harvill Press, 1998) is exactly what it claims to be, but Karl Menninger, *Number Words and Number Symbols. A Cultural History of Numbers* (Dover, New York 1992; Constable & Co. Ltd in the U.K.) is far more relevant, and explains how the Romans coped so efficiently with their own letters-as-numerals arithmetic. What we find in Insular Biblical style, inherited and sometimes modified from the *arithmetica* of St Jerome's Vulgate and Roman schooling, is a late manifestation of a much older and much more complicated scheme of proportions and symbolic numbers found in Hebrew and Greek; for this, see John Michell, *The Dimensions of Paradise* (Thames & Hudson, 1988).

The Penguin Classics translations of Ovid and Plautus have been mentioned in the *References*. The best Latin text, with full notes and vocabulary, of Ovid's *Metamorphoses*, XI, is G. M. H. Murphy's edition, originally O.U.P., Oxford, reprinted 1979 by Bristol Classical Press. The comedies of Plautus have attracted any number of translators, some of whom capture the speed and humour (most do not), and the standard texts remain those in the O.U.P.'s Oxford Classical Texts series. By far the best version of the *Menaechmi* is J. B. Poynton's *Five Plays of Plautus* (Blackwell's, Oxford 1973).

No separate history of early Anglesey exists; Sir J. E. Lloyd's *A History of Wales* (see n.11) contains the story of the House of Gwynedd from its beginnings until the English conquests. Earlier references to 970 *Catamanus* in *Archaeologia Cambrensis* (=*AC*), not relevant to this study, are: *AC* n.s., I (1846), 160–9, H. L. Jones on Llangadwaladr church, depiction of slab with George Petrie's correct reading; same vol., 302ff., notes by J.O.Westwood; *AC* 6th ser., XVIII (1918), 182, Sir John Rhys, "has long since been moved from its old position ... to another inside wall"; and *AC* 7th ser., IV (1924), H. H. Hughes, valuable discussion of the letter-forms. And lastly, those who are insufficiently familiar with Conan Doyle's writing may like to know that in his *Sherlock Holmes Long Stories*, chap. 2 of "A Study in Scarlet" and chap.1 in "The Sign of Four" are both entitled "The Science of Deduction". In the second, despite having just injected himself with a seven-per-cent solution of cocaine, Holmes distinguishes – brilliantly – between *observation* and *deduction*.